I Luvs Ya

They Do Not Understand Series

Patricia C. Vines

Copyright @2016

Patricia C. Vines

All rights reserved. No part of this book may be reproduced or transmitted in any form or by any means, electronic or mechanical, including photocopying, recording, or by any information storage and retrieval system, without permission in writing from the copyright owner or author.

The information in this book is for educational purposes only.

ISBN-13: 978-1518885402
ISBN-10: 1518885403

First Edition
Published; January 2016
Printed in the United States of America

Table of Contents

Introduction iv
Acknowledgments vii
I Luvs Ya 1
The Creation Verbs 4
Man's Portion in Life 12
The Creation of the Man's Body 18
The Need for a Counterpart 21
Adam's Spine 23
The Spine Returns 25
The Protection of Companion Man, Companion Help Woman 28
What Men Need to Do 39
Three Principles of Authority 44
Man's Badge of Authority 46
The Woman's Badge of Submission 48
Man, the Glory of God 51
Woman, the Glory of Man 51
Hair – The Long and the Short of It 53
Fulfillment of Companion Man, Companion Help Woman 57
The Discernment of Doctrine 58
The Demonstration of Nature 59
The Significance of Woman's Long Hair 61
Bible Doctrine, Guardian of the Soul and Body 63
King David – Bathsheba 64
The Divisive Woman 71
Pathway to Destruction 74
Avoid Temptation – WOW!! 76
The Consequences of Promiscuity 78
The Prohibition of Adultery 81
The Man's Aggressiveness 86
Blessing of Companion Man, Companion Helper Relationship 87
The Perfect Balance 90
The Slavery of Promiscuity 91
The Bride of Christ 93
A Heart like Jesus 95
7 Feast of the LORD Being Symbolic of New Life ... 97

Introduction

There have been many gifts that have blessed my life – the first one was "Grace" of conversion (Salvation) to Yeshua, my Savior. The other gifts were my family, my children, my Grandchildren and Great Grandchildren, my friends and then as life's path seemed filled with things that make the going rough, and I wished for a smoother road, when I felt like I had had enough.... I paused a moment and remembered "Who's" in charge, Yeshua.

I prayed a prayer, never really expecting it to be answered. Yeshua sent a man into my life that loves Him (Yeshua) as much if not more than I do. I did not ask for tall, short, thin, fat, rich or poor. Like a lightning bolt - he appeared. His compassion, love, friendship has and is making his and mine an amazing journey. The hills that loom ahead no longer seem so large, when we know we are not alone. He has opened doors I never imagined possible to grow, to face each journey through the sheer wisdom he has shared and shown, to know that God will guide and give the strength to win. That it is not about being right, but about getting it right.

I have learned from Yeshua that "God is the master craftsman – He is the potter and man the clay. God is the mason – man the stone. God is the smith – man the pliable metal. God is the captain – man the rudder. God is the weaver – man the warp and spun into many aspects of life.

Yeshua has shown me that the "Torah" makes up the written traditions of a Jewish nation. That GENESIS stands as one of the great literary and spiritual classics of all civilization. That EXODUS is the great tribal epic of liberation, its main role occupied by Moses, one of history's great personalities, at first impetuous & dangerous, next reluctant & stammering, and transformed again to be both PATIENT & DECISIVE. That LEVITICUS is the book of the Levites, or the priestly tribe of Israel. It lays out the detailed social & religious code by which Israel is to be governed. That NUMBERS (named for the census taken at Sinai) is better titled in Hebrew as BEMIDBAR or "In the Wilderness." this is the book of years of wandering. Then DEUTERONOMY (The Second Law) is mainly taken up with Moses' final addresses to the people, expounding on the 10 Commandments and preparing them to enter into the Promised Land. It ended with a beautiful eulogy to the great prophet "whom the LORD knew face to face."

Yeshua has taught me to "Shema" - listen and obey. Obeying has never been a problem, but listening is another matter. Our modern Western culture tends to focus on mental activity. "It is the thought that counts," or so we think. But biblical cultures are very action-oriented, and this is reflected even in the language. Many verbs that we consider mental activities (hearing, knowing, remembering, etc.) are broadened to include their physical outcomes as well. Understanding this is often a great help for Bible study.

An excellent example is the word "Shema". It has a primary meaning of "hear" or "listen". Listening in our culture is considered a mental activity (communication, almost a lost art) and hearing means that our ears pick up sounds. But in the Bible, the word SHEMA is widely used to describe hearing and also its outcomes: understanding, taking heed, being obedient, obey the words one hears – the result of listening & doing what is asked. Take heed! Listen and obey! Love God with all of your life! For knowing this helps us discover the fuller meaning of my book – I Luvs Ya. Hebrew also lacks abstractions, so interesting physical images are used to express abstract idea. Without an abstract word for "stubbornness," the people are described as "stiff-necked"; and without a word for "stingy," people are described as "tight-fisted." We can easily hear the thoughts in these expressions.

Knowing the greater meaning of SHEMA "obey" helps us understand why Yeshua (Jesus) says, "He who has ears to hear, let him hear!" He is calling us to put his words into action, not just listen. He wants us to be doers of the word, and not hearers only (James 1:22). Western thinking stresses the exercise of the intellect and tends to minimize the DOING of the Word – even viewing this as "dead works". But Hebrew thinking emphasizes that we have not truly taken what we have heard into our hearts until it transforms our lives as well. It is our relationship to him (Yeshua). Henceforth, my book "I Luvs Ya" and lessons about life, those wanting not only deeper intellectual understanding, but wanting to grow into more joyful & deeper discipleship, a marriage relationship of companion man and companion helper woman and a 'how to' manual.

This book is the first in a series called "They Do Not Understand". Most of our problems stems from the fact that we do not understand so many things. This book and the books which are to follow will address this challenge that every one of us face.

It's not about being right; it's about getting it right!

Acknowledgments

GOD'S WORD® Translation is a registered trademark of GOD'S WORD® to the Nations, PO Box 400, Orange Park, Florida 32067-0400.

"Scripture quotations taken from the New American Standard Bible®, Copyright© 1960, 1962, 1963, 1968, 1971, 1972, 1973, 1975, 1977, 1995 by The Lockman Foundation Used by permission." (www.Lockman.org)

Scripture quotations are taken from the HOLY BIBLE, New Living Translation, copyright© 1996, 2004, 2007, 2013 by Tyndale House Foundation. Used by permission of Tyndale House Publishers, Inc., Carol Stream, Illinois 60188. All rights reserved.

Some of the Scripture quotations, in this publication are from the HOLY BIBLE, NEW INTERNATIONAL VERSION® NIV® Copyright© 1973, 1978, 1984, 2011 by Biblica, Inc.®. Used by permission. All rights reserved worldwide. The "NIV" and "New International Version" are trademarks registered in the United States Patent and Trademark Office by Biblica, Inc.®. Use of either trademark requires the permission of Biblica, Inc.®.

"Scripture quotations are from The Holy Bible, English Standard Version® (ESV®), copyright© 2001 by Crossway, a publishing ministry of Good News Publishers. Used by permission. All rights reserved."

Scripture quotations marked HCSB are taken from the Holman Christian Standard Bible®, Copyright© 1999, 2000, 2002, 2003 by Holman Bible Publishers. Used by permission. Holman Christian Standard Bible®, Holman CSB®, and HCSB® are federally registered trademarks of Holman Bible Publishers.

Scripture taken from the New King James Version®. Copyright© 1982 by Thomas Nelson, Inc. Used by permission. All rights reserved.

All pictures and information contained therein in this book is factual to the best of the authors information and is presented for informational and entertainment purposes only.

I Luvs Ya

Like any story to fully understand and get the bigger picture, we need to start at the beginning.

The God of Israel is the God of Jesus – Divine Love and Divine Wrath is written and explained throughout Scripture. Genesis Chapter 1 & 2 contains the story of creation. The first account of men and women were created simultaneously. God set up a decree and it is a pronouncement that has and will always exist:

Genesis 1:26;
26 And God said, "Let us make man in our image, after our likeness; and let them have dominion over the fish of the sea, and over the fowl of the air, and over the cattle, and over all of the earth, and over every creeping thing that creepeth over the earth."

"God" in Genesis 1:26, is a plural word in the Hebrew – ***ELOHIM*** – primarily it designates God as God. *El* means *mighty* or *strong*. ***Elohim*** is the primary word translated GOD in the Old Testament.

He is the creator of all things, "all things have been created by Him and for Him" (Colossians 1:16).

We are a unique creation of God, one of a kind, created for His glory. He "didst form my inward parts." He "didst weave me in my mother's womb....I am fearfully and wonderfully made."

Psalm 139:13-14;
13 For thou hast possessed my reins: thou hast covered me in my mother's womb.
14 I will praise thee; for I am fearfully *and* wonderfully made: marvellous *are* thy works; and *that* my soul knoweth right well.

Have you ever thought of yourself as being fearfully and

wonderfully made? Or do you look at yourself and despise what Elohim has created. Why would God create people who are different from His normal pattern of creation?

The first significance in Verse 26, the word "God said" indicates that the Members of the Trinity held a conference, and what they decided at that conference is a part of the plan. The subject on the agenda is "man." but specifically, the principle of *COMPANION MAN – COMPANION HELPER WOMAN.* This has been a discussed topic in time, but much more so in heaven. At the time that the Father, the Son and the Holy Spirit decided to create man and woman they also decided to provide for the male of the species a companion helper woman, and apart from a few exceptions, every person who has ever lived has – by divine design and by God's grace – a right companion counterpart.

Genesis 1:27;
27 "So God created man (refers to souls – multiple people) in his *own* image, in the image of God created he him, male and female created he them."

In Genesis 1:28 He (man) is commanded to "subdue" - acquire a knowledge and mastery over his material environment, to bring its elements into the service of the race.
The second significance of the phrase "God said" is this: **COMPANION MAN – COMPANION HELPER WOMAN WAS GIVEN/PROVIDED HISTORICALLY BEFORE SALVATION.** Originally man have no sin and therefore had no need of salvation; so the greatest thing God ever did for the human race, apart from salvation, was to make provision for Companion Man – Companion helper Woman. God provided for the male and female in every realm of their relationship with God (Trinity), their physical relationship, and their soul relationship. The first man and woman had a marvelous/perfect spiritual life with Jesus Christ personally.

He taught them "Bible Classes" every evening in the cool of the Garden.

Genesis 3:8;
8 And they heard the voice of the LORD God walking in the garden in the cool of the day: and Adam and his wife hid themselves from the presence of the LORD God amongst the trees of the garden.

In this day and time people are constantly seeking happiness in such things as status symbols, cars, materialistic things, wealth, social life, large elegant homes, relaxation or privacy, in security or success. At one time or another, everyone has wished for the "pot of gold" at the end of the rainbow. Yet ultimately, with the exception of a spiritual relationship with the Lord, having your companion man or your companion helper woman is the most perfect of human happiness. God has designed this fantastic happiness on earth for both believers and unbelievers. Some have experienced this happiness, while many others have missed it.

Many of us still have some illusions about life, but you are also beginning to see many things which are false. Now the word of God is designed to correct all of that through the reading, studying and obeying Torah (the first five books of the Old Testament) as it is on the basis of the Word of which I'm going to set forth certain principles – in order that you can have a FANTASTIC RELATIONSHIP SPIRITUALLY, PHYSICALLY AND SOULISHLY with a person designed for you – even though everything else in the world may be going wrong, you find comfort in each other.

I realize that this may be a delicate subject to some of you, but I will begin with GOD. This is always a good place to start, because it will help to lessen many of the problems. When you understand something of God's viewpoint – it cannot be wrong!!! GOD IS PERFECT – HIS DESIGN, HIS PLAN and HIS PROVISIONS are **PERFECT!!!** Apart from salvation and spiritual provisions, both of which are salvation, spiritual, grace gifts, God has even provided some other things that are absolutely perfect. There's one woman in the world perfectly suited for every man; there is one man perfectly suited for every woman – just one – not two, not three, not a dozen. Please keep in mind that there are exceptions such as being a widow, widower, etc. One may have tried a dozen and already reached this conclusion. However, in arriving at this conclusion, one may have also done great damage to oneself with regard to the possibility of fulfilling the divine design. Like the other grace gifts, sex must be understood within the framework of Divine Design (Love). God, who designed this for our happiness, also set up laws and boundaries. They are: Laws of Marriage; Laws of Divorce; Laws of Levirate Marriage and Release; Laws of the Virgin Maiden; Laws of a Woman Suspected of Adultery.

In the nature of an animal, there is no such thing as "right stud" or "right bitch." A male animal seeks the company of ANY female animal and vise-versa. Like the animal nature, the OLD sin nature in the human species is frequently not particular. Therefore, due to the distortions of the sin nature, it is impossible to determine apart from Scripture, what God has ordained and what man has corrupted.

The Creation Verbs

And God said, "Let us make man....." There are four (4) Hebrew verbs which are used in placing man and woman on this earth in their physical bodies & with souls

1. BARA.......... To make something out of ***nothing***; the creation of the invisible ***essence*** (image) and spirits inside their bodies.
Genesis 1:27;
27 "So God created man in his own image, in the

image of God created he him; male and female created he them."
Genesis 5:1-2;
1 This is the book of the generation of Adam. In the day that God created man, in the likeness of God made he him."
2 "Male and female created her them; and blessed them, and called their name Adam, in the day when they were created."
Isaiah 43:7;
7 "*Even* every one who is called by my name; for I have created him for my glory; I have formed him; yea, I have made him."

2. ASAH.......... To manufacture something out of existing materials. (Your personality is a manifestation of your soul)
Genesis 1:26;
26 And God said, "Let us make man in our image, after our likeness; and let them have dominion over the fish of the sea, and over the fowl of the air, and over the cattle, and over all the earth, and over every creeping ting that creepeth upon the earth."
Isaiah 43:7;
7 "*Even* every one who is called by my name; for I have created him for my glory; I have formed him; yea, I have made him."
Isaiah 57:16;
16 "For I will not contend forever, neither will I be always angry for the spirit should fail before me, and the souls *which* I have made."

3. JATSAR.......... Used for the creation of the male body only. (Ish)
Genesis 2:7;
7 "And the Lord God formed man of the dust of the

ground, and breathed into his nostrils the breath of life; and man (became) a living soul."

4. BANAH.......... Used for the creation of the female body only. (Ishad or Ishah) "And the rib (Hebrew word for column, for stands upright) which the Lord God had taken from man, made he a woman, and brought her unto the man."

BARA refers to one aspect of the soul – essence – indicated by the word "image." BARA is the invisible essence of your soul and consists of self-consciousness, mentality, volition, emotion and conscience. All of these together make up a distinct personality.

ASAH emphasizes another aspect of the soul – personality. ASAH is not used for the physical part of man, but is used in connection with BARA for the creation of the soul and the human spirit. Although ASAH means "to manufacture something out of something," it actually has to do with human personality. You see, your personality is a manifestation of your soul.

Everyone – male and female – has the same characteristics of the soul. All of us have mentality – a left and right brain. We have a conscience in our right brain; with our volition we have the ability to make decisions; and to have emotions with which to appreciate things in life and with which to respond. The old sin nature, which is also a part of the soul, was not created and therefore is not an issue at this point. God has manufactured – out of the essence of our souls – a distinct personality which belongs only to the individual. So we have two words used for the creation of the human soul, because there are two parts to the soul of man – essence and personality, as man is a personality.

"And ELOHIM said, Let us ASAH (manufacture) man...." Now we have an interesting thing: the word "man" is ADAM in the Hebrew, the given name for one man is "ISH."

Here is another distinction which you should learn. The word ADAM, by itself, always refers to male and female – that is, multiple people or human race. It is the same concept as homo sapiens, or mankind. There is another word for "man" - HA-ADAM. This Hebrew form includes the definite article. HA-ADAM is not the human race in general but refers to the first man and the original creation by GOD. This distinction is not the human race in general but refers to the first man and the original creation by God. This distinction always occurs in the original Hebrew. So the literal translation here, "ELOHIM said, Let us manufacture out of the essence (something that is) of the soul, the HUMAN RACE.

ELOHIM is the key to understanding the words "image" and "likeness." Although Jesus Christ is the actual Creator;

John 1:3;
3 "All things were made by him; and without him was not anything made that was made."

Colossians 1:16;
16 "For by him were all things created, that are in heaven, and that are in earth, visible and invisible, whether *they* be thrones or dominions, or principalities, or powers – all things were created by him, and for him....."

Hebrews 1:10;
10 "And, Thou, Lord, in the beginning hast laid the foundation of the earth; and the heavens are the works of thing hands."

He is not mentioned here (that will come up later under "Jehovah Elohim") since this is still the planning stage. The plural ELOHIM is used to indicate the identical essence of God the Father, God the Son, and God the Holy Spirit. There is a pattern here: just as ELOHIM is one in essence, so man – male or female – has the same essence of soul. But there is also a difference, and the difference comes from the fact that there are three separate and distinct Persons in the Godhead –

therefore – three Personalities. Just so, there are many, many separate and distinct individuals in the human race and as many bona fide personalities.

"Image" and "likeness" refer to invisible essence. "Image," TSELEM in the Hebrew, is "shadow image" or "essence." Should someone open your head and look inside, he would not find self-consciousness or thoughts; he could not see volition, emotion, norms and standards or the conscience. These things are TSELEM – they are real but invisible, just as God is real but invisible. Actually the word TSELEM has a first person plural suffix, which indicates all three Members of the Godhead. All three have essence, but their essence is invisible.

John 1:18;
18 "No man hath seen God at any time; the only begotten Son, who is in the bosom of the Father he hath declared *him.*")

You cannot see it with the eye – and it is intangible – you cannot handle or touch it.

The exact same thing is true of man. God made an invisible part of man which is the REAL MAN. The REAL YOU is the SOUL! Just as God has invisible but real essence, so man, though in a different way and in a limited sense, has invisible and intangible but real essence.

The second word, "likeness," or DEMUTH, is a model or pattern. This means that just as all three Members of the Godhead have the same essence and are three separate and distinct Persons, so every member of the human race has the same essence (that which makes something what it is), but we all have different personalities – we are separate persons.

Genesis 1:27;
27 "So God (ELOHIM) created man in his *own* image, in the image of God created he him, male and female created he

them."

"Created" here is BARA – to create something out of nothing. Now I want you to notice what it says: He created HA-ADAM – the man, one specific person. Verse 26 refers to the human race in general, and verse 27 refers to Adam in particular. And then again we have the fact that he was created in the image of God. This is, of course, TSELEM. The first Adam had "essence."

Now something is a little different is added: "MALE & FEMALE created he THEM." First, this indicates that the male and female became living creatures at separate times. "Male" - ZAKAR – refers to the male soul of Adam, which was created on the sixth day and activated according to this verse.

Genesis 2:7;
7 "And the Lord God formed man *of* the ground, and breathed into his nostrils the breath of life; and man became a living soul."

Activation involved the provision of a body to house the soul. You see, the soul of every human being must have a "house", and God actually provided on Day-plus-6, the day He created man, a house for the male only. Please note, that the female was in incubation inside Adam awaiting the time God would provide a house for the female soul and she would actually become a living person.

"Female" - NEQEBAH – refers to the woman with regard to her soul, which was designed to respond to man under the concept of companion man – companion helper woman. We discover the details in Genesis Chapter 2. After Adam was created (Mr. Name all the Animals) he was alone for an extended length of time. We are not given the exact time, but he found NO help fit for him – no female to match him as all else were in pairs. In fact, it states this in the following verse.

Genesis 2:19;
19 "And out of the ground the Lord God formed every beast of the field, and every fowl of the air; and brought *them* unto Adam to see what he would call them: and whatsoever Adam called every living creature, that was the name thereof."

Adam had been given a "GREAT INTELLIGENCE" and he went to work as instructed by God the Son– still without woman, because since Day-plus-6 man had a body, a soul and a spirit; but woman did not exist as a person until sometime later, as we shall see in a rather dramatic way. Thus, there was a period on the earth when there was only one male of the species – in fact, that will become an issue very shortly. So, "Male and female created he them" indicates that although both souls were created at the same time, only one (1) body, only one (1) person was truly alive. The woman's soul was still in incubation – the original "SLEEPING BEAUTY" - WAITING TO BE KISSED BY THE PRINCE UPON HER ARRIVAL IN THE GARDEN OF EDEN.

In the day that God created man, in the likeness of God made he him (HA-ADAM, the first man), the book of generations began.

"In the day" refers to Day-plus-6. "Created" - BARA – (something out of nothing), the word used for the essence of the soul. On the sixth day, man's body, soul and spirit were created; the woman's soul was "bara'd" but not activated. "In the likeness" (DEMUTH – a model or pattern) refers to their personalities. Again we have a reference to the entire human race, but the emphasis is on the creation of man with different kinds of personalities. "Made" (ASAH – means to manufacture personalities out of invisible essence). The last word "him" (OTHO – refers to the souls of both the man and the woman. Both of their souls were created on Day-plus-6, but one was activated and one was not.

Genesis 5:2;
2 "Male and female created (BARA) he them; and blessed them and called their name Adam (human race) in the day when they were created."

Adam is the natural head of the human race.

Luke 3:38;
38 "Who was *the son* of Enos, who was *the son* of Seth, who was *the son* of Adam, who was *the son* of God.

Although the word "male" here indicates the male sex, it is used for man's soul, which was designed to satisfy the soul of the female under the concept or mind set of companion man – companion helper woman. "Female" is used for the soul of companion helper woman, which was designed to respond to the companion man.

Here are the categories of love.

Category one, toward God.
Category two, toward man or companion.
Category three, toward friends.

Category two (stated above) starts in the soul and overflows to the body. The souls of companion man – companion helper woman, as well as their bodies, are designed to be a perfect match for each other; but it is discovery in the soul that leads to the eventual intimacy of the bodies.

Genesis 5:2 adds something else **"and blessed them."** All men that hate women should realize that the design of one male soul and one female soul under Category Two love is the first and greatest blessing that man can ever receive apart from salvation! It is intensive, indicating tremendous happiness – the ultimate of human happiness. The following verse portrays a beautiful illustration of this principle.

Man's Portion in Life

Ecclesiastes 9:9;
9 "Live joyfully with the wife whom thou lovest all the days of the life of thy vanity, which he hath given under the sun, all the days of they vanity; for that *is* thy portion in *this* life, and in thy labor which thou takest under the sun."

Man's Portion in Life
"Enjoy life with the wife you have loved throughout your meaningless life that he has given you under the sun, all the days of your futility, for that is your alloted portion in life and in your labor that you work at under the sun.
or
See (enjoy) living with the companion helper woman whom thou hast loved all the days of your life of emptiness, whom he has given you under the sun – all the days of emptiness; for this companion, helper (woman) is your portion in life, and in your work (occupation) in which you are working under the sun.

"Live joyfully" as translated in the English is weak. What it actually says is more intriguing and just as good!!! First of all, there is no verb here for "live"; the word is a COMMAND and means "to see and enjoy." See and enjoy what? **SEE LIVES! ENJOY LIVES!** "Lives" refers to all the capacities of the soul and body. The rest of the verse explains in what connection this command is to be fulfilled. First of all, it is referring to a male believer, and he is to see and enjoy the soul and body of his Companion helper woman whom he loves. "Hast loved" (1 Corinthians 13 – I Luvs Ya) means that he experiences that love in time, although it was designed in the past. It is the strongest word in the Hebrew language for love – Hebrew, AHAB.

"All the days" refers to the remainder of their lives after the Companion Helper woman is brought to the Companion man. Every time a Companion man is with his Companion Helper woman, it's an entire lifetime of blessing! And this is true even though his life is otherwise filled with "Vanity" (emptiness – a term denoting the life of the unbeliever). Companion helper woman is a gift of grace, for the believer and unbeliever alike, during the time in which they are alive on planet earth. God did not intend for man to be miserable with a life of emptiness / loneliness. God intended every man to have a COMPANION HELPER WOMAN! For the unbeliever, this is the only true or lasting happiness he an ever have. This concept KNOCKS out every type of perversion.

1. Homosexuality – Sexual desire for those of the same sex.
   Ecclesiastes 7:28-29;
   28 "Which yet my soul seeketh, but I find not: one man among a thousand have I found, but a woman among all those have I not found."
   29 "Lo, this only have I found, that God hath made man upright, but they have sought out many devices."

2. Lesbianism – Sexual practices of homosexuality between women.
   Romans 1:26;
   26 "For this cause God gave them up unto vile affections, for even their women did (exchange) the natural use for that which is against nature."

3. Bestiality – Depraved, vile sexual act between humans and animals.
   Leviticus 18:23;
   23 "Neither shalt thou lie with any beast to defile thyself therewith; neither shall any woman stand

before a beast to lie down thereto, it is confusion."
Leviticus 20:15-16;
15 And if a man lie with a beast, he shall surely be put to death: and ye shall slay the beast.
16 And if a woman approach unto any beast, and lie down thereto, thou shalt kill the woman, and the beast: they shall surely be put to death; their blood *shall be* upon them.
Leviticus 21:15;
15 "Neither shall he profane his seed among his people, for I, the Lord, do sanctify him."
Deuteronomy 27:21;
21 "Cursed be he who lieth with any manner of beast. And all the people shall say, Amen."

4. Masturbation – To practice genital self-excitation – auto-erotism, also called self-abuse.
   1 Corinthians 6:18;
   18 Flee fornication. Every sin that a man doeth is without the body; but he that committeth fornication sinneth against his own body.

5. Adultery – Violation of the marriage bed; sexual intercourse between a married man and a woman not his wife, or between a married woman and a man not her husband. Also, includes Mental Adultery.

Exodus 20:14;
14 Thou shalt not commit adultery.
Matthew 5:28;
28 But I say unto you, That whosoever looketh on a woman to lust after her hath committed adultery with her already in his heart.

Persons who are inclined toward any form of sexual perversion (sin) inevitably deprive themselves completely and totally of this one type of happiness in life – Companion man – Companion helper woman.

"If" - there are four (4) meanings for the word "If" as follows:

1. "If" and it's true.
2. "If" and it's not true.
3. "If" - maybe yes, maybe no.
4. "If" - I wish it were, but, it's not.

"If" - 1 John 1:9 - "IF" we confess our sins, he is faithful and just to forgive us our sins, and to cleanse us from all unrighteousness."

If Elohim designed this gift (male and/or female) so that even an unbeliever with an empty life can have happiness, IMAGINE how it will add up for the believer in Yeshua with Bible knowledge who gets hold of the same thing! A believer will not only have salvation and happiness with Elohim forever, but he also has two other gifts from God which provide happiness in time – Scripture Bible Doctrine and Companion helper woman. Of course, adverse spiritual conditions such as a failure to mature spiritually that causes **SCAR TISSUE,** (the concept or mental attitude thinking that causes "hardening of the heart." It's negative thinking toward God or Bible Doctrine that puts scar tissue on the soul – the heart becomes "hardened" toward God and doctrine. Searching for happiness in the following:

1. Promiscuity – An indiscriminate mixture especially in sexual relations.
   Galatians 5:19-21;
   19 Now the works of the flesh are manifest, which are *these*; Adultery, fornication, uncleanness, lasciviousness,
   20 Idolatry, witchcraft, hatred, variance, emulations, wrath, strife, seditions, heresies,
   21 Envyings, murders, drunkenness, revellings, and

such like: of the which I tell you before, as I have also told *you* in time past, that they which do such things shall not inherit the kingdom of God.
2. Drug Addition – A habitual use of narcotics or habitual inclination.
Revelation 21:8;
8 But the fearful, and unbelieving, and the abominable, and murderers, and whoremongers, and sorcerers, and idolaters, and all liars, shall have their part in the lake which burneth with fire and brimstone: which is the second death.
3. Alcoholism – A diseased condition caused by the excessive or continuous use of alcoholic liquors.
Proverbs 20:1;
1 Wine *is* a mocker, strong drink *is* raging: and whosoever is deceived thereby is not wise.

Or any other frantic search for happiness that is sin and puts scar tissue on the soul – there is no capacity for a relationship with other people or with God the Father, God the Son, or God the Holy Spirit. No desire to abide by the Law of Torah or the Commandments. REVERSIONISM: a believer rejects the true objects of love and enters into false love and relationship which causes self induced misery. In other words, doing the opposite of God's plan for our life. REVERSE PROCESS REVERSIONISM: This is the function of a reversionistic believer that rejects true objects of love and enters into the above mentioned states plus more (an opposite direction) and becomes negative toward the Law of Torah, in other words, an emotional revolt, a mental attitude that produces sin that causes self-induced misery.

Proverbs 15:13;
13 "A merry heart maketh a cheerful countenance, but by sorrow of the heart the spirit is broken,"

It destroys the capacity for true happiness. "For this is YOUR PORTION in life" refers to the fact that God has given to everyone a portion of happiness – believer or unbeliever. There is not a homosexual walking the streets today for whom ELOHIM did not provided a Companion helper woman. There is not a lesbian in this world today that ELOHIM did not provide a Companion man. In this day and time many have missed the boat so to speak, through perversion, just as many will miss the boat of salvation. Depending on ones volition (act of will). **One can miss all of ELOHIM's GRACE PROVISIONS OR ONE CAN HAVE THEM. GRACE IS THE EMPOWERING TO GET THE JOB DONE.**

The phrase "and in your occupation in which you are working under the sun (in life)," is a reference to an additional source of enjoyment in life which Elohim has provided – your profession and or occupation. According to the following verses, man has two portions in life:

Ecclesiastes 9:9;
9 "Live joyfully with the wife whom thou lovest all the days of the life of thy vanity, which he hath given thee under the sun, all the days of thy vanity; for that is thy portion in *this* life, and in thy labor which thou takest under the sun."

Elohim gives man work – by the sweat of his brow – and a Companion helper female. This is an absolutely awesome thought. For every male and for every female there is a "**I Luvs ya**", **a companion counterpart.** Every person on the face of the earth, now or at any time in history, who is in any kind of perversion (wrong mind set) – sexual or spiritual – has missed or purposely bypassed Elohim's portion for amazing happiness. Interestingly, Noah had one Companion helper as did Joseph, Moses, Joshua and Samuel, and there may have been others of which we are not made aware. They all had their Companion Husband's back and were unto him a Comfort, Counterpart and a Completor. They knew that to have multiple wives under one roof would cause jealousy, example, Joseph wives (Gen. 29, 30); Elkanah's wives (1 Samuel 1:6); Gideon's misery caused trouble among his children (Judges 9); David's misery compounded the problem in the children and discipline carried to the 2nd generation (1 Chron. 3:1-9). They did not follow laws set up by God for the protection, orderly function and survival of the human race during the conflict of angels. (Genesis 6).

This should really tell us that it adds up to something – that we cannot loose with Bible Doctrine, reading, studying Torah and abiding by the Commandments. Doctrine provides the capacity with which to recognize and appreciate the Companion Man – Companion Helper woman, and God knows just the right time to bring along your chosen Companion Man or Companion Helper woman. He provides everything at just the right time, but Scripture, Torah, is the avenue of appreciation, the avenue for understanding, and the avenue for a relationship with God which leads to this wonderful principle of "I Luvs Ya" of Companion man and Companion Helper woman.

The Creation of the Man's Body

Genesis 2:7;
7 "And the Lord God formed man *of* the dust of the ground, and breathed into his nostrils the breath of life and man became a living soul."

(Corrected translation of Genesis 2:7 below)

"Then ADONAI, GOD (Jehovah Elohim) formed a person (Hebrew – Adam) from the dust of the ground (Hebrew – Adamah) and breathed into his nostrils the breath of life, so that he became a living being."
Complete Jewish Bible

There is a change from ELOHIM in Genesis 1:26, 27, to JEHOVAH ELOHIM. (Note: One of the names for God is ELOHIM. Primarily it designates God as God. Deuteronomy 10:17 says, "Jehovah your Elohim is God of gods....*El* means *mighty or strong* and is used for any reference to gods, including Almighty God. *Elohim* is the primary word translated *God* in the Old Testament. 'Sometimes *Jehovah* is translated *God* rather than *LORD*.' The *him ending* of Elohim is very significant, for it is a plural ending in the Hebrew that indicates three or more. Elohim, the name for God as Creator, is used in Genesis 1:1 and thus "could" be translated, "In the beginning Gods created the heavens and the earth." Does this mean that there was more than one God? NO! "The LORD (Jehovah) is our God (Elohim). The LORD is one" (Deuteronomy 6:4). It was God the Father, God the Son, and God the Holy Spirit, the Trinity Who created the heavens and the earth. One in essence, in character, yet three persons united as one. As we read various Scripture, we can see references to the different persons of the Godhead participating in the work of creation.

Genesis 1:2-3;
2 "The Spirit of God was moving over the surface of the waters.
3 Then God said, 'Let there be light'; and there was light."
Hebrews 11:3;
3 "By faith we understand that the worlds were prepared by the word of God"

God spoke; the Spirit moved; and Colossians 1:16 tells us that in Him, in Jesus Christ, the Son, "all things were created, both in the heavens and on earth".

Colossians 1:16;
16 "For by him were all things created, that are in heaven, and that are in earth, visible and invisible, whether *they* be

thrones or dominions, or principalities, or powers – all things were created by him, and for him....."

Thus, we see that each person of the triune Godhead had a part in creation. This is seen even in the creation of man, for in Genesis 1:26 we read, "Then God (Elohim) said, 'Let Us make man in Our image.'" The "US" has to refer to more than one!!!) It is well to note that the Members of the Godhead are all involved. Jehovah is a name and is sometimes used for the Father, sometimes for the Son and sometimes for the Holy Spirit. But it is always a reference to a specific Member of the Trinity, which is determined by the context. Essence is found in ELOHIM: Personality is found in JEHOVAH. Jehovah here refers to Jesus Christ. He is separate and distinct from the other Members of the Godhead, as they are from Him. But, since His essence is exactly the same as the Father's and the Holy Spirit's, He is called JEHOVAH ELOHIM.

Jesus Christ forms – JATSAR'S – man. The creation of man's soul and personality, remember was BARA and ASAH and a body on Day-plus-6, now, man gets a body, not anybody, but the body to house the soul and personality. The verb JATSAR (to fashion) is used for the creation of man's body in contrast to the creation of the woman's body, coming much later under the word BANAH (to build). "Man" as you might guess, is HA-ADAM, but he will shortly receive another name. He will become known as ISH. However, there can be no ISH because there is no ISHAH. In all the garden he will not find a match for himself. He is going to be extremely LONELY until he receives the gift of ISHAH. When he receives the gift of ISHAH he will change. HA-ADAM will become ISH because ISH has his ISHAD!! After all, a man can only watch birds and animals so long before he begins to get lonely for another of his kind. That's the whole point coming up in verses 18 and following. So "JEHOVAH ELOHIM formed HA-ADAM (specific man) out of the dust of the ground." "Dust" is EPHER; but note, the ground is called ADAMAH. ADAM (the human race), HA-ADAM (the first man) and ADAMAH (ground) all have the same general relationship. The dust of the ground can be the chemicals in the soil or any other construction material existing at that time in the ground which God used to form the body of man. It was a fantastic body, but it still wasn't "cranked up." Let's take a look at what the body of the man looked like: He was considered to be the "Chiefest among 10 thousand not yet made – He was like Lebanon, excellent as a Cedar, tall and sturdy. His accountancy was white and ruddy. His hair was bushy, curly, purple black or red or blond. His eyes were the eyes of doves, large, fitly set with thick curly lashes, color of brown, hazel, blue – drop dead gorgeous eyes. His lips were like Henna flowers, speaking blessings and joy, altogether lovely. His Cheeks were like bed of spices, dimples in cheeks and chin and salty to the taste. His mouth is sweet, it is like apples dipped in honey, like cakes of raisins, sweet smelling myrrh. His teeth, white and evenly spaced. His legs are like pillars of marble set in sockets of fine gold, muscle, pure muscle. His hands, strong, like steel and velvet. His voice, tender with spoken words, firm and deep if needed. He is like a fountain of water, powerfully flowing upward and gracefully falling....

The Need for a Counterpart

Genesis 2:19-20;
19 "So from the ground ADONAI, God, formed every wild animal and every bird that flies in the air, and he brought them to the person to see what he would call them. Whatever the person would call each living creature, that was to be its name"
20 "So the person gave names to all the livestock, to the birds in the air and to every wild animal. But for Adam there was not found a companion suitable for helping him. Complete

Jewish Bible

We could imagine that Adam (Mr. Name all the Animals) spent a hundred or so years within the garden (zoo) watching and naming all those animals. Supposedly the last name he would give was ISHAH. He would watch as he taught her and then gave her a name, too. But first he had a job to do. He had to "catalog" creation – that is, he had to give a name to all that God had created. Now here's the problem: **"but for Adam there was not found a help met for him."** "Help meet" is literally **"a help over against"** him – a counterpart (female), or a help responding to him.

We need to notice what did NOT exist in the state of innocence. Category Three love! Only Category One and Category Two love existed before Sin entered the world. Between the Companion Man and the Companion Helper woman, there is only Category Two love. It is the only love in which physical contact is bona fide. Category Three is NON-TOUCHING! That should tell everyone who ever has a tendency toward any perversion of God's design that when things are absolutely perfect no one ever thought of anything but Categories One and Two love. (Category One Love is toward God – Category Two Love is toward Companion Man and Companion Helper Woman and Category Three Love is toward Friends.)

Is it actually Jesus Christ speaking in the above listed verses? He said, **"Not good"** that man should be alone. This refers to the man being without a woman. This was the conclusion of a perfect Person, Jesus Christ.

Everything man has seen so far in lower creation had a counterpart – an opposite member. There was a male and a female in every species, no matter what it was. This undoubtedly caused Adam to become increasingly aware that he was the only male that was completely alone! So ADONIA, Jesus Christ says, **"I will make (ASAH-manufacture) for him a help met (a help responding to** him)."

Adam's Spine

Genesis 2:21;
21 "Then God caused a deep sleep to fall upon the person; and while he was sleeping, he took one of his ribs and closed up the place from which he took it with flesh." Complete Jewish Bible

The deep sleep is equivalent to an anesthetic so that Adam would not feel any pain. The Lord Jesus Christ actually performed the operation. The woman's soul, remember had already been manufactured. It's the body of the woman that requires the procedure. Although there are other verbs which could have been used for "took," it is interesting that the verb LAQACH is used here. This means in the Hebrew **"to seize violently."** The woman was pulled violently out of Adam and violently (passionately) she returns to him! It's almost like being pulled apart and coming together demonstrates a fantastic passion. It indicates something of the magnetism and the passion which exists between Companion man and Companion helper woman.

"He took out one of his ribs" or **"one from among his ribs."** Did Adam have two spines or columns, side by side? The word for **"ribs"** is very interesting. It's the feminine noun **TESLAH**; but it has a third masculine singular suffix indicating that, although the rib actually belonged to Adam, it was a feminine rib inside him all that time. **TESLAH** is not the usual word for rib. **TESLAH** is ordinarily the word for a **beam** or a **joist** of a building. It is used this way in

1 Kings 6:15-16;
15 "The insides of the walls of the house he built with boards of cedar: from the floor of the house to the joist of the ceiling he covered them with the inside with wood, and he covered the floor of the house with boards of cypress."

16 "The thirty-five-foot back portion of the house he built with boards of cedar from the floor of the joists and reserved this part of the house to be a sanctuary, the Especially Holy Place."

1 Kings 7:3;
3 "It had a roof made of cedar and supported by beams lying on forty-five posts, fifteen in a row."

In connection to the Companion helper woman, this usage is very appropriate. Then Jesus Christ closed up the hole with flesh.

Genesis 2:22;
22 "The rib which ADONIA, God had taken from the person, he made a woman-person and brought her to the man-person."

Note: In the hands of the Lord Jesus Christ a rib (spine), and that significant act, which occurred many thousands of years ago, still has and always will have good and bad repercussions. It is a very dramatic moment, because when Jesus Christ was holding that rib (spine), he was actually holding bone that would bring either great happiness or great unhappiness (misery) to the human race. The Companion man may have a miserable or horrible life, but if he has his Companion Helper woman, he has great happiness with her. It's a marvelous GIFT of grace.

This grace gift is for the entire human race, yet the entire human race does not benefit. There are unbelievers and believers who never have their Companion man or Companion Helper woman. There are also members of the human race that do not benefit from the second grace gift of salvation. God provides perfectly, but both gifts require human mind set.

Part of Adam is now missing, and out of the missing part Jesus Christ made (BANAH) a woman. The Hebrew word

BANAH is very interesting: it actually means TO BUILD. The woman's body was BUILT! The man's body was fashioned – JATSAR. There's a difference. The woman has a body that is different from anything else in creation. It is fantastic! A house was constructed for the woman's soul, and God put that soul into it. Please note – God continued to follow the same procedure of allowing Adam to identify and name all of the species. The word for woman here is actually the name which Adam will give her – ISHAH. ISHAD is one of the Hebrew words that apply to her body.

Then God / Jesus Christ "brought her unto the man," or literally, He brought her to HA-ADAM. Right here is the beginning of the principle of Companion man – Companion Helper woman. *God designed the woman perfectly for the man. He seized violently (passionately) the rib out of Adam and left a gap which is only fulfilled by that which He BUILT.* Then He caused her to be brought to HA-ADAM. That's the way it still is! If people will wait ad observe the laws of divine establishment, God will provide. And this is a provision for unbelievers as well. That's why the laws of divine establishment (These laws are principles set up by God for the protection, orderly function, survival of the human race during the period of the angels conflict – Genesis Chapter 6) forbid certain practices of fornication, homosexuality, bestiality and autoerotim (self-generated sexual activity such as masturbation). If practiced, any and all of these things get man off the track, and hereby cause him to lose his capacity for the greatest happiness in life – apart from salvation and Bible doctrine, study and obedience to the laws of Torah and the Commandments.

The Spine Returns

Genesis 2:23;
23 "The man-person said, "At last! This is bone from my bones and flesh from my flesh. She is to be called Woman

(Hebrew: ISHAD), because she was taken out of Man (Hebrew: ISH)."

Jesus Christ has a marvelous (great) sense of humor. He brought the woman for Adam to name in much the same way He had brought the animals. Jesus Christ probably said, **"What are you going to call his one, Adam?"** Now Adam being a man of great intelligence, looked and it only took a couple of seconds to realize that he had his counterpart. **She was absolutely beautiful.** And guess what he called her. ISHAD! Woman! And ISHAD she was and ISHAD she is. One ISHAD issued to one ISH – no more, no less. Perfect issue - "P.I." Adam knew that his words would feed her soul. He compared her to a company of horses – strong – glistening!! She was fair with eyes of Doves as pools of water. Her lips were threads of scarlet – sweet like honey – speech is comely as honey and milk are under her tongue. Her neck like a tower of ivory or chains of gold. Her hair, curly, purple black, thick, or possibly red or blond. Her teeth are even and pearly – one beside the other – evenly spaced. Her mouth drips wine, sweet. Her temples are like pomegranates. Her breast like lilies clusters of grapes.

Her thighs are like jewels, the hands of a skilled workman and her feet are beautiful. She is a garden – a well of living water – supernatural and overflowing when warmed and becomes bubbly. Her fragrance is an ointment of myrrh perfume – the fragrance of Lebanon. Adam gives her roses with dew and the fragrance flows off on her – a marvelous aroma.

There is a woman whose soul and body are perfectly designed for you and no one else will do – ever. That statement should scare one!! A lot of persons think that God said, "Thou shalt not commit ......," because He did not want you to have any fun. To the contrary, God said it because he WANTED people to have fun FOR LIFE! If you are an unbeliever, the greatest enjoyment/fun you will ever have is here on earth with a woman – your Companion Helper woman, because you are going to spend an eternity in hell.

John 3:36;
36 "Whoever trusts in the Son has eternal life. But whoever disobeys the Son will not see that life but remains subject to God's wrath."

Accept the Gift of God, His Son, Obey Torah, and the Commandments. Please note that if a believer looses their spouses to death, then God has in reserve another Companion man and a Companion Helper woman, as it is not good for man to be alone. (Together, a man and a woman are a special unit, stronger together than either alone.

Ecclesiastes 4:9 & 12;
9 Two *are* better than one; because they have a good reward for their labor.
12 And if one prevail against him, two shall withstand him; and a threefold cord is not quickly broken.

Just think, BELIEVERS who find their Companion Helper woman, whether they are spiritual or carnal, have all of this and heaven, too! God designed woman to be the quintessence of happiness for man. But He did not design EVERY woman to be the essence of our happiness – just one or upon death, another.

Now before Adam named her, he did some explaining. He said, "This now," or literally, "this one, she." There is no verb here. A verb at a time like this is not needed. Remember, Jesus Christ is binging to him the most PERFECT, BEAUTIFUL woman ever formed. She does not have a thing on and neither does Adam. It absolutely took his breath away when he saw her! Please note that he has not touched her yet. You do not know why that's important? The identification was made IN HIS SOUL! But the identification was very, very physical, even though as yet he had had no physical experience. Does that tell you something? It should tell one that when one finds the one who is absolutely right for him or her, the physical aspect of your relationship presents no problem at all.

"This one, she, bone from my bones" - Adam knew that something was missing in his life and that this woman would complete him. What was missing would come back with GREAT INTEREST! So he adds, "flesh from my flesh, this one, she, shall be called ISHAH." Why, because she was taken out of ISH!

He had not felt a thing when she was seized violently/passionately from him; and now that he sees what Jesus Christ has made from his rib/spine, Adam realizes that he has what is called the "GRAND PASSION."

There is an interesting switch here: the word for "man" is no longer HA-ADAM; now we have ISH. Why? Up until this time, man has been alone. He was created incomplete and can be completed only by the woman. Once the woman is brought in, they become ISH and ISHAH. When ISHAH is taken from ISH, ISHAH becomes one with ISH; (NOTE) He fulfills her and she completes him. The Companion man and the Companion Helper woman is the most perfect sex relationship that ever existed.

The Protection of Companion Man – Companion Helper Woman

Genesis 2:24;
24 This is why man is to leave his father and mother and stick with his wife, and they are to be one flesh.

There are four (4) ways of acquiring a body:

1. Without man or a woman as Adam did – made from the dust of the earth.
2. With a man, but no woman – as Eve was made from Adam.

3. With a man and a woman, as all humans are born.
4. With a woman – but no man – as Jesus was born. Having an earthly Mother, but no biological father.

Every baby is a being that never existed before.

Isaiah 7:14;
14 "Therefore *Adonai* himself will give you people a sign: the young woman will become pregnant, bear a son & name him 'Immanu El (God is with us).

Adam does not have a mother and a father, but the principle must be set up now. Outside of volition (the actual act of the mind of the power which the mind has for considering an act of the will). "Adonai, God, gave the person this order.

Genesis 2:16-17;
16 'You may freely eat from every tree in the garden'"
17 "except the tree of the knowledge of good and evil. You are NOT to eat from it, because on the day that you eat from it, it will become certain that you will die."

There was only one other principle of establishment in the Garden of Eden at this time – Companion Man and Companion Helper woman. The framework for THIS marriage – monogamy. Now that the Companion Man and the Companion Helper woman are in the Garden, something must be designed to protect their relationship. What is going to keep man, WHO IS THE AUTHORITY IN THIS RELATIONSHIP, from eventually turning into a tyrant?

God protects the woman from the tyranny of the man, who has the authority over her, by adding the laws of establishment – the family or parents – to accompany the principle of Companion Man and Companion Helper Woman. While marriage is the protection of woman – man must learn to love and respect for the woman. This rule was never established in the animal kingdom, or even in the angelic creation – only in the human race. Both the father and mother have a contribution to make to teach a boy to have respect for womanhood, so that when his own woman comes into his life, their relationship will be the ultimate in happiness. There are also laws of Torah as stated: "The Book of Holiness" - Groups of laws are three – Laws of Forbidden Sexual Relations, Laws of Forbidden Foods, Laws of Slaughter. (Listed are only the Laws of Forbidden Sexual Relations):

These are in Leviticus 18.

1. Not to have sexual relations with one's Mother.
   Leviticus 18:7;
   7 The nakedness of thy father, or the nakedness of thy mother, shalt thou not uncover: she *is* thy mother; thou shalt not uncover her nakedness.
2. Not to have sexual relations with one's father's wife.
   Leviticus 18:8;
   8 The nakedness of thy father's wife shalt thou not uncover: it *is* thy father's nakedness.
3. Not to have sexual relations with one's sister.
   Leviticus 18:9;
   9 The nakedness of thy sister, the daughter of thy father, or daughter of thy mother, *whether she be* born at home, or born abroad, *even* their nakedness thou shalt not uncover.
4. Not to have sexual relations with one's father's wife's daughter.
   Leviticus 18:11;
   11 The nakedness of thy father's wife's daughter, begotten of thy father, she *is* thy sister, thou shalt not uncover her nakedness.
5. Not to have sexual relations with one's son's daughter.
   Leviticus 18:9;
   9 The nakedness of thy sister, the daughter of thy

father, or daughter of thy mother, *whether she be* born at home, or born abroad, *even* their nakedness thou shalt not uncover.
6. Not to have sexual relations with one's daughter.
Leviticus 18:10;
10 The nakedness of thy son's daughter, or of thy daughter's daughter, *even* their nakedness thou shalt not uncover: for theirs *is* thine own nakedness.
7. Not to have sexual relations with one's daughter's daughter.
Leviticus 18:17;
17 Thou shalt not uncover the nakedness of a woman and her daughter, neither shalt thou take her son's daughter, or her daughter's daughter, to uncover her nakedness; *for* they *are* her near kinswomen: it *is* wickedness.
8. Not to marry a woman and her daughter.
Leviticus 18:17;
17 Thou shalt not uncover the nakedness of a woman and her daughter, neither shalt thou take her son's daughter, or her daughter's daughter, to uncover her nakedness; *for* they *are* her near kinswomen: it *is* wickedness.
9. Not to marry a woman and her son's daughter.
Leviticus 18:17;
17 Thou shalt not uncover the nakedness of a woman and her daughter, neither shalt thou take her son's daughter, or her daughter's daughter, to uncover her nakedness; *for* they *are* her near kinswomen: it *is* wickedness.
10. Not to marry a woman and her daughter's daughter.
Leviticus 18:17;
17 Thou shalt not uncover the nakedness of a woman and her daughter, neither shalt thou take her son's daughter, or her daughter's daughter, to uncover her nakedness; *for* they *are* her near kinswomen: it *is*

wickedness.
11. Not to have sexual relations with one's father's sister, **Leviticus 18:9;**
    9 The nakedness of thy sister, the daughter of thy father, or daughter of thy mother, *whether she be* born at home, or born abroad, *even* their nakedness thou shalt not uncover.
12. Not to have sexual relations with one's mother's sister. **Leviticus 18:13;**
    13 Thou shalt not uncover the nakedness of thy mother's sister: for she *is* thy mother's near kinswoman.
13. Not to have sexual relations with one's father's brother's wife. **Leviticus 18:14;**
    14 Thou shalt not uncover the nakedness of thy father's brother, thou shalt not approach to his wife: she *is* thine aunt.
14. Not to have sexual relations with one's son's wife. **Leviticus 18:15;**
    15 Thou shalt not uncover the nakedness of thy daughter in law: she *is* thy son's wife; thou shalt not uncover her nakedness.
15. Not to have sexual relations with one's brother's wife. **Leviticus 18:16;**
    16 Thou shalt not uncover the nakedness of thy brother's wife: it *is* thy brother's nakedness.
16. Not to have sexual relations with one's wife's sister. **Leviticus 18:18;**
    18 Neither shalt thou take a wife to her sister, to vex *her*, to uncover her nakedness, beside the other in her life *time.*
17. Not to have sexual relations with an animal. **Leviticus 18:23;**
    23 Neither shalt thou lie with any beast to defile thyself therewith: neither shall any woman stand

before a beast to lie down thereto: it *is* confusion.
18. That a woman shall not bring an animal to have sexual relations with her.
Leviticus 18:23;
23 Neither shalt thou lie with any beast to defile thyself therewith: neither shall any woman stand before a beast to lie down thereto: it *is* confusion.
19. Not to have sexual relations with another male.
Leviticus 20:13;
13 If a man also lie with mankind, as he lieth with a woman, both of them have committed an abomination: they shall surely be put to death; their blood *shall be* upon them.
20. Not to have sexual relations with one's father.
Leviticus 18:7;
7 The nakedness of thy father, or the nakedness of thy mother, shalt thou not uncover: she *is* thy mother; thou shalt not uncover her nakedness.
21. Not to have sexual relations with one's father's brother.
Leviticus 18:14;
14 Thou shalt not uncover the nakedness of thy father's brother, thou shalt not approach to his wife: she *is* thine aunt.
22. Not to have sexual relations with another man's wife.
Leviticus 18:20;
20 Moreover thou shalt not lie carnally with thy neighbour's wife, to defile thyself with her.
23. Not to have sexual relations with a menstrous woman.
Leviticus 20:18;
18 And if a man shall lie with a woman having her sickness, and shall uncover her nakedness; he hath discovered her fountain, and she hath uncovered the fountain of her blood: and both of them shall be cut off from among their people.
24. Not to intermarry with Gentiles.

Deuteronomy 7:1-3;
1 When the LORD thy God shall bring thee into the land whither thou goest to possess it, and hath cast out many nations before thee, the Hittites, and the Girgashites, and the Amorites, and the Canaanites, and the Perizzites, and the Hivites, and the Jebusites, seven nations greater and mightier than thou;
2 And when the LORD thy God shall deliver them before thee; thou shalt smite them, *and* utterly destroy them; thou shalt make no covenant with them, nor shew mercy unto them:
3 Neither shalt thou make marriages with them; thy daughter thou shalt not give unto his son, nor his daughter shalt thou take unto thy son.

25. That an Ammonite or Moabite shall not enter the community by marriage with born Jews.
Deuteronomy 23:3;
3 An Ammonite or Moabite shall not enter into the congregation of the LORD; even to their tenth generation shall they not enter into the congregation of the LORD for ever:
26. Not to keep an Egyptian of the third generation from so entering the community.
Deuteronomy 23:7-8;
7 Do not despise an Edomite, for the Edomites are related to you. Do not despise an Egyptian, because you resided as foreigners in their country.
8 The third generation of children born to them may enter the assembly of the Lord.
27. Not to keep an Edomite of the third generation from so entering the community.
Deuteronomy 23:7-8;
7 Do not despise an Edomite, for the Edomites are related to you. Do not despise an Egyptian, because you resided as foreigners in their country.
8 The third generation of children born to them may

enter the assembly of the Lord.
28. That a mamzer shall not so enter the community.
   Deuteronomy 23:2;
   2 No one born of a forbidden marriage[a] nor any of their descendants may enter the assembly of the Lord, not even in the tenth generation.
29. That a eunuch shall not so enter the community.
   Deuteronomy 23:1;
   1 He that is wounded in the stones, or hath his privy member cut off, shall not enter into the congregation of the LORD.
30. Not to castrate a male, even a domestic animal or wild beast or fowl.
   Deuteronomy 22:24;
   24 Ye shall not offer unto the LORD that which is bruised, or crushed, or broken, or cut; neither shall ye make *any offering thereof* in your land.
31. That the High Priest shall not marry a widow.
   Leviticus 21:14;
   14 A widow, or a divorced woman, or profane, *or* an harlot, these shall he not take: but he shall take a virgin of his own people to wife.
32. That The High Priest shall not have sexual relations with a widow, even without marriage.
   Leviticus 21:14;
   14 A widow, or a divorced woman, or profane, *or* an harlot, these shall he not take: but he shall take a virgin of his own people to wife.
33. That the High Priest shall marry a virgin in her adolescence.
   Leviticus 21:13;
   13 " 'The woman he marries must be a virgin
34. That a Priest shall not marry a divorced woman.
   Leviticus 21:14;
   14 A widow, or a divorced woman, or profane, *or* an harlot, these shall he not take: but he shall take a

virgin of his own people to wife.
35. That he shall not marry a harlot.
Leviticus 21:14;
14 A widow, or a divorced woman, or profane, *or* an harlot, these shall he not take: but he shall take a virgin of his own people to wife.
36. That he shall not marry a profaned woman,
Leviticus 21:7;
7 " 'They must not marry women defiled by prostitution or divorced from their husbands, because priests are holy to their God.
37. That one shall not be intimate with one with which sexual relations are severely forbidden.
Leviticus 18:6;
6 None of you shall approach to any that is near of kin to him, to uncover *their* nakedness: I *am* the LORD.

The Laws of Forbidden Foods and Laws of Slaughter shall not be listed at this time.

The young man first learns the principles of authority and respect for women from his mother, he learns by example from his father. The father also must provide security, protection, discipline, and some training, but the first teacher in the human realm is the mother. Both the father and mother are mentioned, but the father is mentioned first because he's the authority in the home. It is the responsibility of parents to teach the boy to become a gentleman, so that when he is a man, he will not be an "ANIMAL."

A boy's/man attitude toward his mother often determines what he will be like with the Companion Helper woman. If the father treats the mother well, the boy/man will usually follow his example. The sad thing in today's society is that so many children are not learning authority and respect from their mothers, and fathers are setting an example of brutality. As a result, the children never see the gentleness and the tenderness that can exist between a man and a woman. A boy/man reacts to this, and his reaction is always an ANIMAL reaction: he often becomes promiscuous, brutal, or even a rapist.

First, there is love for womankind when a young boy/man loves and respects his mother. This gives him both the perspective and the training to fulfill his Companion Helper woman without abusing his God-given authority under the order of – God the Father, God the Son, God the Holy Spirit, MAN, woman, children, servant. Please note, that a man's respect for his mother must never be a hindrance when it's time for him to leave his mother and father to enter into a new relationship. This greatest relationship of his life is described in the next phrase, "**and shall cleave (be intimately united) unto his ISHAH (woman).**" There is no word for "wife" in the Hebrew language. The trouble with the word "wife" is that today we tend to connect it with a wedding ceremony and all its regalia – yet it's very simple – HIS ISHAH! HIS WOMAN!

The word "cleave" translated means - "to stick, to adhere, to be attached, to cling, to be glued to" but in this context it means "**sexual relationship!**" That's exactly what it is. It's a new relationship. When as an adult you leave the influence of the home, you move into a relationship which is first of all the soul, but it is also of the body. The male and female bodies were designed for that. IT'S AMAZING, AFTER ALL THESE THOUSANDS OF YEARS, THE DESIGN HAS NOT CHANGED. The woman is still a woman, and the man is still a man – Thank God!

When this verse was quoted in the New Testament, the word "cleave" was translated "JOIN."

Ephesians 5:31;
31 "For this cause shall a man leave his father and mother, and shall be joined unto his wife, and they two shall be one flesh"

Please note, the Greek word **PROSKOLLAO** is not joined – it's something no animal could ever do. It's face-to-face sex! The man and the woman shall be intimately united in sex, and they are one flesh. God has violently/passionately pulled the rib/spine out of Adam, built a fantastic woman, and then passionately brought her back to Adam! Now here's the point: they began their physical relationship as an expression of Companion Man and Companion Helper woman love.

Genesis 2:25;
25 "They were both naked, the man (companion) and his wife (companion, helper) and they were not ashamed (confused or disappointed).

ISH (man) and **ISHAD** (woman) did not have any clothes. The first time they put on clothes (that represented clothing) they were the wrong clothes (fig leaves). Scripture tells us that God made for them coats of skins (sheep skin). They were not ashamed, confused, or disappointed prior to the fall. They did not have any hang-ups about their physical appearance or relationships. There was no such thing as perversion where the Companion man or Companion helper woman were concerned – Hebrews 13:4 "Marriage is honorable in every respect; and, in particular, sex within marriage is pure. But God will indeed punish fornicators and adulterers. Anything to which Companion man and Companion helper woman **BOTH** agree is **NOT** perversion! That brings us to "Harmony and Music of Marriage".

If there is to be music of marriage in the home then:

1. The man sings – leads.
2. The woman harmonizes with the man.
3. They sing the songs together.

The man is the provider. The woman is the helper. The man is the protector. The woman is the nurturer – she brings beauty and enhancement to the home. God made man and woman different in order that they are one.

We live in a society with a generation of kids extremely mixed up. But not all are mixed up. An example is the "Rooster saw a plate of scrambled eggs and he said to the hen, "Honey, there are our crazy mixed up children."

Children do not know if they are being raised by feminine men or masculine women – midget miniature men brought on by radical feminists.

We need a society of mature masculine men. According to Ephesians, Chapter five (5) there are five (5) things men must do. This chapter is much tougher on men than women. We are experiencing divorce, homosexuality, emotional distress, suicide, etc. because the men have chosen to be irresponsible. Here is a list of what men must do:

What Men Need to Do

Men Must Assume Responsibility

Ephesians 5:25;
25 Husbands, love your wives, even as Christ also loved the church, and gave himself for it;

There is no chain of command, only chain of **RESPONSIBILITY, TO BE THE HEAD IS TO BE RESPONSIBLE.** Men are the head, not the tail. In 1 Corinthians 11:3 the head of the man is Christ. God is the head of Christ. Man exists to meet **NEEDS.** Woman is to look to her husband's leadership to be the servant leader and to be submissive is not to be inferior. In Phil. 2 we are to take on the form of servant (slave) – like Jesus when we have a submissive spirit, we are not to be like satan and be rebellious or violent. Christian submissiveness – one equal to another – voluntarily placing one's self under the authority of another so that Christ (God) can and will be glorified.

There is no "Partnership" in Marriage.

In a partnership there is no head. They must be a **"TEAM"**. The husband calls the plays as the "COACH" says that he is in charge of the home. Someone has to do it and therefore, it's better for everyone to be going in the same direction than each going his or her own separate way. The husband may delegate **"AUTHORITY"** to the woman such as writing checks, etc., but if there is failure in the system, the husband is still **RESPONSIBLE,** NOT the woman. If there is to be respect and trust, they must be earned; therefore, the man should shoot for respect as trust will come automatically. It is a safety net for the woman to respect the headship of her husband.

The Husband Must Let His Wife Know That She Is Number One (1) In His Life.

She comes before the children, before his mother, before his father, etc., that she is number one (1) of all human beings in man's life. It is security to know that one (1) person loves me more than all others on this earth. The same applies to her concerning her husband. The husband is to treat her as Christ treated the Church. Most men are not guilty of sexual adultery, but of **EMOTIONAL** adultery and emotional adultery is a crime and a sin against God.

Man Needs To Protect His Wife From Emotional Trauma.

Ephesians 5:26-27;
26 to make her holy, cleansing her by the washing with water through the word,
27 and to present her to himself as a radiant church, without stain or wrinkle or any other blemish, but holy and blameless.

We have two (2) words: **SPOT OR WRINKLE.** They

mean to protect her from emotional trauma and/or damage.

SPOT means trash, refuse, dirt, no dumping allowed on wife. He does not need to be the guy who dumps on her but he needs to let her know where he hurts in order that she can pray and weep with him, as she is number one (1) in the husband's life.

WRINKLE means or speaks of an **INTERNAL-TRAUMA-PAIN**. It will always show on face, showing sadness. The husband is not to be a midget man. The husband is to be masculine and is to protect his wife. It is his assignment to make his wife more radiant and beautiful!

The Husband Is Make His Wife Feel Secure, Nourished And Cherished.

Nourishment is to give food and drink, to help one to grow, to feel cherished. Cherished is to warm with body heat, like a hen sits on her eggs and leaves for no reason. It is to nourish with body heat, to hold her. To hold, nourish and cherish her. A husband took his wife to a psychiatrist as his wife was extremely depressed and unresponsive. The psychiatrist determined that the woman should be hugged and kissed. He approached the man's wife, hugged and kissed her and told the husband that was what she needed every day of the week, as her response to the hug and kiss was health warming and she responded. The husband said that was wonderful, but that he could only bring her six (6) days a week, but not on Thursday. The husband just did NOT UNDERSTAND. Women are emotional creatures and men are realistic.

Husbands Are To Take The Initiative.

The Husband is to love his wife as Christ loved the church. As Christ came out of the "Ivory Palaces" into a world of woe, only his great eternal love made our Savior go (come to earth). Revelation 3:20 says behold "I" stand at the door and know.... the man is the initiator and the woman is the responder.

Song of Solomon Chapter 1:8 is the "Music of Marriage:"

Song of Solomon Chapter 1:8 & 15;
8 If thou know not, O thou fairest among women, go thy way forth by the footsteps of the flock, and feed thy kids beside the shepherds' tents.
15 "Fairest art thou among women, though art fair – Dove's eyes.
Song of Solomon 4:1;
1 "Behold thou art fair."
Song of Solomon 5:2;
2 "She is asleep and her 'heart' awaketh... he's knocking at the door...been up all night trying to get to her....
Song of Solomon 5:5;
5 "Her heart goes thump, thump, all this time she is putting on perfume as she wants to be persuaded...

The Husband is to Take the Initiative – If Not, She Will Be Hurt...

Proverbs 7:10;
10 And, behold, there met him a woman *with* the attire of an harlot, and subtle of heart.

The mark of a harlot is that she takes the initiative. The attire of a harlot is dressing as a harlot. She is not a keeper of a home, she is loud mouthed, foolish, stubborn, mulish, she catches him and kisses him. Feminist have and are becoming the initiator.

The Proverbs 31 woman dresses herself beautifully in all ways. Christ demands as much purity from man as he does woman. Man is goal oriented and the courtship should not end with the marriage ceremony.

Man is to Assume Masculinity And Responsibility.

He gives the wife authority, but the man must be responsible. When this occurs then she will be to her husband:

A COMFORT....
A COUNTERPART.....
A COMPLETOR....

There will be harmony in the home.

In 1 Corinthians Chapter 11 we will find further information on the subject of "Adams Rib" or Companion man – Companion Helper woman. In 1 Corinthians 11, two (2) of the greatest grace principles in history are brought together. There are three (3) basic grace gifts from Jesus Christ to the human race:

1. Companion Helper Woman. (He built it – Jesus Christ).
2. Salvation (He did it – Jesus Christ).
3. Doctrine (He thought it – The Word – Jesus Christ).

Under the **first** principle – one companion man for one companion helper woman. Man does not earn or deserve this grace principle. The greatest genius who ever lived could never have thought of such a thing. Even when Adam was categorizing the various creatures, before woman had appeared on the scene, he could not have conceived or devised in his wildest imagination a creature who would completely satisfy the longings of his soul and the desires of his body. Although the Tree (cross) is God's greatest demonstration of grace, the woman is God's walking illustration of grace! She can satisfy everything for which man's soul longs, everything his body desires. She is his **COMPLETION, FULLFILLMENT AND GLORY,**

COMFORT, COUNTERPART AND COMPLETOR.

The **second** grace principle – one companion man for one companion helper woman is illustrated in this passage by the Communion Table, which commemorates the Tree (Cross). Both of these principles were being abused through legalism. All grace gifts are attacked vigorously by satan, and legalism is one of his methods. The legalists had said that the woman had to wear veils in the church. While women did not have hats in the ancient world, they did have veils, and no woman ever went outside without some sort of a veil covering her head. However, there were two kinds of women who were not permitted to wear veils – the prostitutes and the **SLAVES**. Of course, prostitutes and slaves were coming to church in Corinth (which was the center of prostitution in the Roman Empire). Remember, positive volition (self-will) toward Scripture (Bible doctrine) resides in many kinds of people. When these women walked in with their hair uncovered, the legalists immediately became critical. They wanted to throw these women out simply because they were not following the general culture (custom) of the day. Their bullying was causing a lot of trouble for those who were positive toward Bible doctrine, 1 Corinthians 13 (love).

The last half of the chapter (vs. 17-34) is concerned with believers coming to the Lord's Table in a state of intoxication. This was abuse of obedience, reverence to God the Father, God the Son and God the Holy Spirit. Some men/women wear jewelry such as a cross – which is a symbol of grace. Women who wear long hair is also a symbol of grace, but, those who do not have long hair is no less blessed with grace than those who do. It's a matter of the HEART! In the first grace gift, Jesus Christ gave woman to man – Note: GAVE WOMAN TO MAN, not the other way around and the second grace gift Jesus Christ GAVE HIMSELF TO MANKIND!

Three Principles of Authority

1 Corinthians 11:3;
3 "But I intend to have you know, that the head of every nobleman (believer) is the CHRIST; and the head of the woman, THE MAN; the head of Christ, THE GOD"

The verse above is quoted from a literal translation of the original Greek text.

1. **Authority of Christ:**
   Paul begins, not by setting the church straight on the subject of a hat or a veil on the head of the woman, but by teaching three (3) basic principles of authority. The **first** of these is the authority of Jesus Christ. The word for **"head," KEPHALE,** is used quite extensively in the next two verses, and it means **"the head on the shoulders of the human body: - i.e., the residence of the soul and the spirit."** But it also means **"superior rank or authority."** The head contains the brain (as we know) and other factors which control and dictate the functions of the human body. **"Man" - (ANER) – is man in the noble sense – hence, a believer, either male or female.** The superior rank over every believer is **CHRIST**, who is the head of the church.

   Colossians 1:16-18;
   16 For by him were all things created, that are in heaven, and that are in earth, visible and invisible, whether *they be* thrones, or dominions, or principalities, or powers: all things were created by him, and for him:
   17 And he is before all things, and by him all things consist.
   18 And he is the head of the body, the church: who is the beginning, the firstborn from the dead; that in all *things* he might have the preeminence.

2. **Authority of Companion Man:**
   Authority in the church leads to authority in the realm of

Companion Man – Companion Helper woman relationship. While this relationship applies to both believers and unbelievers, we will cover it from the stand point of believers only, according to this passage, and apply Bible doctrine to the situation. In the phrase, **"and the superior rank over the woman, the man,"** there is no verb, which places great emphasis on the principle discussed. From the point of the creation of homo sapiens, the man was recognized as the HEAD of the body called the "WOMAN." Read 1 Corinthians Chapter 11.

3. **The Authority of the Father: "And the head of the Christ, the God," is God the Father.**
The authority of the Father over the Son refers to Jesus Christ in union (the God-Man) during His incarnation.

John 3:16;
16 God so loved the world (people), that He gave his only begotten Son.....

God the Father had the authority and the rank during the incarnation of Christ. That is why Jesus said, **"Father, if thou be willing, remove this cup from me: never the less NOT MY WILL (the will of Jesus Christ IN HIS HUMANITY), but THINE (the sovereignty of God the Father) be done" (Luke 22:42).**
Now the application is brought into the function of the early church, where two illustrations are used – PRAYING AND PROPHESYING. Let's remember 1 Corinthians 13 (LOVE).

Man's Badge of Authority

1 Corinthians 11:4;
4 "Every nobleman praying or prophesying having something down over his head, dishonors his head.

Here "every man" is used for a male believer only, in contrast to the female believer in the next verse. "Praying and prophesying" are both part of the worship service, although prophesying today is only bona fide through the teaching of the Word of God in many passages. Up to now, the word, "head" has been used for superior rank; but it now changes to mean the LITERAL HEAD, by the addition of a prepositional phrase in the Greek, **KATA** and **KEPHALES**. The man has something down over **(KATA)** his literal head **(KEPHALES)**. In that terminology of that day, what does that mean? It means **LONG HAIR**.

A man wears short hair if he's a man in his thinking. Hair style on a man is strictly a matter of what he **THINKS... THINKS... THINKS!** It all comes from the soul. If he's something other than a man who has his hair long because some doll told him he looked good that way, obviously is a responder. He has all the male accouterments, but he's a "woman" in his soul. A man is to be the AUTHORITY over the woman, and the badge is his **SHORT HAIR!** The woman's badge of submission is her longer hair.

People often ask, "What are the signs of the times?" And they expect a dissertation on the Jews going back into the Land or something on the Communist conspiracy. But the signs of the times today are reflected in the male's long hair. Long hair reflects confusion, rebellion and rejection of the laws of AUTHORITY. How long is long hair on a male? "Down over the head" is the standard for man's hair, according to this verse. A good rule of thumb would be that if you can comb your hair so that it comes down over your eyes or nose, its tooooooooo long! It's a veil! And that's exactly the way "veil" is used here, though you can't find the word "veil" in the English – only in the Greek. Long hair, or ever a hat on a man's head in a church service, covers up his AUTHORITY as a man.

If a man's wife has hair shorter than her husband's, it indicates that she dominates – she is the aggressor, and this principle has been violated. Hair is the sign. One may have thought that hair was designed only for beauty, and this is partly true for woman. The most beautiful thing God ever built was the woman, and her hair is her visible glory. However, it is also designed to be her badge of submission to her companion man.

Now, when a male believer prays or prophesies having "something down over his head," he dishonors his head. I really love the humor here. **"Something down over his head," KATA KEPHALES,** is something over his **LITERAL** head; but he dishonors his **KEPHALE** – his real head, or his authority! This is what we call a "thought paronomasia," (in other words, to strengthen your own argument, or a play upon words) and in the Greek it is very humorous. The same word is used but it means two different things: head and superior rank, **KATA KEPHALES** indicates that a man is growing his own veil, and it's a disgrace. He disgraces grace! It's actually not a question of how it looks (though it looks like you know what!!!!); the problem is the condition in the soul, and the condition in the soul is wrong. More often than not, long hair is an outward sign of rebellion against God and God's design.

Long hair dishonors the man's authority over the woman; but more than that, he dishonors Jesus Christ. Who designed the woman? Jesus Christ, the **SAME ONE** who went to the tree (cross) and bore our sins! He gave to the man woman. Down through the ages man has rejected the principle of companion man – companion helper woman – through fornication, adultery, homosexuality, autoerotism (self-generated sexual activity directed toward oneself such as masturbation) and or other perversions. Now, let's see this from the standpoint of the woman.

The Woman's Badge of Submission

1 Corinthians 11:5;

15 "But every woman <u>praying</u> and <u>prophesying</u>, (in public) with the head unveiled dishonors her head; for it is one and the same as if she had been shaved"

There is a word in this verse that needs to be examined – **AKATAKALUPTOS.** We will see this word later on without the **"A"**. This is a very rare Greek word in the New Testament. **"A"** indicates a negative; **KATA** means "down," **KALUPTOS,** "hidden" (something down and hidden). "Down and hidden" is a veil, **KATAKALUPTOS** is the veil that goes over the woman's head and face. The addition of **"A"** means literally, "with the head **UNVEILED."** Paul is using a clever piece of sarcasm here. The legalists do not realize that he is not talking about hats or veils, but about hair. He has already set up the thought paronomasia in relation to the man's hair, and when he gets all the legalists nodding, he will lower the boom!

So far, the legalists have been agreeing with everything Paul has said in principle. Now Paul goes on: **"But every woman <u>praying</u> and <u>prophesying</u> (in public) with the head unveiled disgraces her head….."** The legalists are still nodding: **"Amen brother, if a woman isn't veiled, she disgraces her head!"** But what they fail to recognize, because Paul has not actually said it yet, is that the veil is her hair!

The woman's head is covered with hair. God designed her hair, as well as her body, to be different from the man's. Her hair is a sign of submission both to God and to her Companion man. Therefore, the veil is the woman's hair – a veil which nature has provided. But the woman's hair must be longer than a man's, just as the man's hair must be short. In this way, both recognize that God's grace provision of love is well established in the principle. A prostitute is a woman who has rejected the authority of one man and sold her body to any or all; therefore, Paul makes the analogy to the prostitutes of that day who had been branded or punished by the shaving of their heads. It was a sign of disgrace, and it is still the custom today. During World War II women who fraternized with the enemy were subjected to having their heads shaved. Paul is simply in the process of clarifying the criticism and also adding some principles of doctrine with regard to the companion man and the companion helper woman.

1 Corinthians 11:6;
16 "For if a woman is not veiled, let her also have her hair cut short; but <u>if</u> it is shameful for a woman to wear her hair cut short or to have her head shaved, then let her be veiled"

Paul is saying in effect that if a woman does not have long hair so that it hangs down over her face like a veil, then shave it off! Here is his sanctified sarcasm. While the legalists are nodding their heads because they are thinking of literal veils, Paul is getting ready to shock them by saying that the veil is actually the woman's hair! This is a debater's technique as well as sarcasm. It is, of course a bad moment for the woman without veils who are listening to the reading of Paul's dissertation; but he is making a great stand against legalism. The legalists say that a woman is uncovered if she does not wear a veil (today it would be a hat). Paul says that the only way a woman can come to worship and be uncovered is to have her hair shaved off!

The sarcasm is completed but reversed at the end of verse 6. Paul uses two (2) different words for "shave" in this verse. The first, **KEIRO**, means to take some kind of a knife or cutting tool and shave off the hair right down to the scalp. The other, **ZURAO**, means to use the knife edge to cut it down close. So he says, **"If it's indecent for a woman to have her hair cut off or shaved, keep on veiling her."** To the legalists, this still means that she must wear a veil or hat. But Paul is still working up to his coup de grace: the woman's hair is her veil, and it is the sign of her submission to her companion man. The issue is not hats – but doctrine!

Man, the Glory of God

1 Corinthians 11:7;
7 "For a man indeed (nobleman, believer) should not have his head veiled, because he is the image and glory of God, and the woman is the glory of man."
Complete Jewish Bible

Here is the application: **OPHEILO** plus **OUK** plus **KATAKALUPTO - "that which hides the face when it's down"** -comes to mean, **"veil,"** but it is used for anything falling over the head. It is saying, in effect, that a man ought not to have hair long enough to cover his face. We know this from Paul's conclusion in verses 14 and 15. But first he gives the reasons: man exists as the image and glory of God! Now, even though man is fallen, even though he is disobedient and has a sin nature, man still exists; and in a regenerate state he can glorify God under the principle of spirituality. "Image" has to do with the essence of his soul as it came from the hand of God, while "glory" refers to the edification complex of the soul and a grace life, both of which the believer receives through an intake of Bible doctrine. The soul of man is designed to respond to God. When he does so, he GLORIFIES GOD.

The edification complex of the soul is: Is a mature believer, one whom has stored in the human spirit Bible doctrine consisting of five levels: grace; mental attitude; details of life; ability to love God, companion man and companion helper woman and friends and the fifth being happiness.

Woman, the Glory of Man

"Existing" used in a different translation as the image and glory of God; but the woman is the glory of the man is not used in connection with the woman. Man exists as her AUTHORITY; but she **"keeps on being"** under the AUTHORITY of her companion man, and as such, she is the glory of the man. The woman has a soul and a body which are the glory of man. **"Glory"** here indicates the companion helper woman both as a responder to the companion man and as an illustration of God's grace. It is God's grace when any believer has an edification complex as defined above. It is also God's grace when a companion helper woman responds to her companion man. We have two (2) reasons now for the man to have short hair and the woman longer hair – recognition of the AUTHORITY of God, and recognition that God has placed man in AUTHORITY over the woman.

The concept of verse 7 will be continued in verse 13. Verses 8-12 are parenthetical (giving information or explanation) and in this section we will learn some new things about the doctrine of companion man and companion helper woman.

1 Corinthians 11:8;
8 "For man was not made from woman, but woman from man"

The word **"For"** is used to begin a parenthesis (explanation) and to amplify what has just been said. This verse not only states the order of creation, but the order of companion man – companion helper woman at the point of origin. There was an elapse of time before woman emerged from man. Man existed in the Garden of Eden first and that is the point of his having short hair and the woman having longer hair – the recognition of his AUTHORITY and of the first grace gift from Jesus Christ. Jesus Christ violently (passionately) pulled the rib (spine/column) out from the man **(ISH)** and – in all her glory – **ISHAH (woman) came violently/passionately** back to **ISH**.

1 Corinthians 11:9;
9 "....and indeed man was not created for the sake of the woman, but woman for the sake of the man"

The companion helper woman was created for the companion man. Whatever man lacks in shortness of hair, she makes up for it, and although man is the AUTHORITY, he is incomplete. A general may be in command, but he is incomplete without an army. So man, **"wearing his rank on his head,"** is incomplete with **ISHAH**. God did a very humorous thing: He put longer hair on the woman to remind man that, while he has AUTHORITY over her, he is NOTHING without her. He is a little short on hair to remind him that he's a little short without woman – God's companion helper for him – God's grace package in FLESH FORM! The greatest form of human happiness for a woman is to be fulfilled by her companion man, and the greatest in human happiness for a man is to be completed by his companion helper woman. There is nothing to compare with this happiness outside of the spiritual realm.

Hair – The Long and the Short of It

1 Corinthians 11:10;
10 "The reason a woman should show by veiling her head that she is under AUTHORITY (of her companion man) has to do with angels."

EXZOUSIA, mistranslated **"power,"** is always **"AUTHORITY,"** and it is always used in grace principle. It is used here for companion man – companion helper woman. It is used in John 1:12 for salvation:

John 1:12;
12 "But to as many as did receive him, to those who put their trust in his person and power (AUTHORITY - EXZOUSIA), he gave the right to become children of God..." (even to them

that believe on his name)

"Because of this" - because the companion helper woman was designed for companion man.... because of love (companion man and companion helper woman)... because the companion man has AUTHORITY over the companion helper woman.... because the companion helper woman is an empty vessel designed to respond to the companion man – the companion helper woman ought to wear the badge of her design on her head! God designed her head to be covered with the sign that the man is her AUTHORITY. Her head is veiled with longer hair; his head has short hair to show that he is the **HEAD (AUTHORITY)** over the woman!

The extreme shortness of hair on the companion helper woman is a sign of some soul kink, or some hang-up. It is a sign of mental attitude disobedience/sin, reversionism (turning the opposite way) are the greatest enemies of the companion man – companion helper woman relationship. In the practice of reverse process reversionism, the woman fornicates with inconsequential persons. She responds to the wrong man - "operation nymphomania" - she goes for woman - "operation lesbianism"; with animals - "operation bestiality"; or she responds to herself - "operation masturbation." These are all manifestations of reversionism and are perversions of love. This is why a woman condemned under these conditions had her hair publicly shaved in the ancient world.

There is a time in any girl's life when almost anything that wears trousers looks great. Theoretically she gets over that" but all her life she is going to see men that are attractive to her for one reason or another. That is why a woman wears long hair – she is not at the disposal of any man who is attractive to her. There is only one man who is her companion man and that's it – period! A doctrinally oriented woman with longer hair is saying, **"I recognize the grace of God. He has given me a man. I am an empty vessel** without this man. There is only one man that can fulfill me. There is only one man who can turn me on.

1 Corinthians 7:9;
9 But if they cannot contain, let them marry: for it is better to marry than to burn.

The 'burning' of or who can turn her into a true woman – only one man: not a dog, not another woman, not the wrong man, and certainly not an ANGEL!" THOSE ARE PSEUDO-LOVERS (FALSE)!
A woman should wear her hair longer as a reminder to angelic creation as well as to the human race. Women are designed for men of the HUMAN RACE ONLY – not for angels. WHY? Our first clue is found in Genesis 6:1-9.

Genesis 6:1-9;
1 And it came to pass, when men began to multiply on the face of the earth, and daughters were born unto them,
2 That the sons of God saw the daughters of men that they *were* fair; and they took them wives of all which they chose.
3 And the LORD said, My spirit shall not always strive with man, for that he also *is* flesh: yet his days shall be an hundred and twenty years.
4 There were giants in the earth in those days; and also after that, when the sons of God came in unto the daughters of men, and they bare *children* to them, the same *became* mighty men which *were* of old, men of renown.
5 And GOD saw that the wickedness of man *was* great in the earth, and *that* every imagination of the thoughts of his heart *was* only evil continually.
6 And it repented the LORD that he had made man on the earth, and it grieved him at his heart.
7 And the LORD said, I will destroy man whom I have created from the face of the earth; both man, and beast, and the creeping thing, and the fowls of the air; for it repenteth

me that I have made them.
8 But Noah found grace in the eyes of the LORD.
9 These *are* the generations of Noah: Noah was a just man *and* perfect in his generations, *and* Noah walked with God.

The angels had been observing the women and "FLIPPED" over them. Finally, when there was an excess of women during the period before the flood, the angels decided to get into the picture. They made a bargain with the fathers and husbands of these women, promising multiple intelligence of various abilities unknown at the time to men. The Men agreed to give the women to the angels in exchange for the information and at that time the angels had the capability of cohabitation and were able to produce children by means of angelic infiltration into the human race creating hybrids, half angel and half human. These hybrids became the super-heroes of the ancient world, the heroes of Greek and Roman mythology. These supermen – such as Castor, Pollox, Achilles, Hercules, etc., - all had human mothers and "angels" for fathers.

The men failed to recognize the AUTHORITY that God had provided. Of course, the time before the flood was one of the greatest periods of apostasy in human history. God put a stop to the cohabitation of angels and human women after Genesis 6 in order that satan would never be able to use that strategy again to stop the pure blood line of Christ to be born unto our salvation; however, the principle remains because of the angelic conflict. Upon death of the hybrids, there was no place for their spirits (N'filim) to go – not to heaven and not to hell. Their spirits remain here on earth to this day.

Numbers 13:33;
33 "We saw the N'filim, the descendants of 'Anak, who was from the N'filim: to ourselves we looked like grasshoppers by comparison, and we looked that way to them too!"

Reported to Moses, the two whom believed they could take the land **(now Israel)** were Caleb and Joshua.

The Fulfillment of Companion Man – Companion Helper Woman

1 Corinthians 11:11;
11 "Nevertheless, in union with the Lord neither is woman independent of man nor is man independent of woman"

"Nevertheless" is designed to qualify man's AUTHORITY over his companion helper woman. What is the qualification? Man's authority over his companion helper woman was never designed to be a tyranny, but a complete fulfillment. When two (2) become one – companion man and companion helper woman – they are totally dependent upon each other. They will never be anything without the other again. Each individual is incomplete without the other; this is not just a hit-or-miss thing. It is the Lord's design! The only exception to this is the gift or the consecration of celibacy under the principle of supreme sacrifice, as in the case of the apostle Paul.

1 Corinthians 11:12;
12 "for as the woman was made from the man, so also the man is now born through the woman. But everything is from God.
Or
"For just as the woman came (originally) out of man or from the source of man, now, even so also the man through the woman. But all things come out from the source of God...

Just as before the "fall" man was incomplete without his companion helper woman, so after the "fall" man cannot exist without the woman. Since the "fall," man owes his origin, his existence and his fulfillment to womankind. First there is his mother. Then the time comes when the man leaves his mother and father to go to his companion helper woman. Man's fulfillment is from the source of his companion helper woman, first grace gift and then salvation through Jesus Christ – the second grace gift through God. Note: One of the greatest problems in marriage is NOT the woman who "goes home to Daddy or Mother," but the **"BOY"** who never cuts the umbilical cord!

The **"all things come out from the source of God"** here are parents and companion man – companion helper woman, but the emphasis is on the **"all things"** in the life of a man – his mother and his companion helper woman. This is something which is absolutely fantastic – a grace gift from God to the human race. The only thing that keeps man from becoming an animal are two (2) women in his life – his mother and his companion helper woman! With few exceptions, no man in all of history was ever a man without the training of his mother and the fulfillment of his companion helper woman.

This ends the parenthesis, and verse 13 takes us back to the subject of the short hair of the man and the longer hair of the woman.

The Discernment of Doctrine

1 Corinthians 11:13;
13 "Decide for yourselves: is it appropriate for a woman to pray to God when she is unveiled."

Here is an appeal to common sense. Common sense is NOT common to the human race. It is actually the bridge between God's revelation (not previously known) and the knowledge of Bible doctrine which we have assimilated (absorbed) through grace understanding. "Discernment" is the application of Biblical common sense to any situation.

Now women like to be "proper or appropriate" to a specific purpose. Is it proper or appropriate for a woman to pray to God unveiled? And here is that rare word again – **AKATAKALUPTOS** – something that hangs down so that it hides the face. In other words, is it proper or appropriate to pray without longer hair? If a woman has her hair cut above her ears, it is usually a sign that she has already rejected God's order and design. Therefore, if she is in rebellion toward God, common sense tells you that her prayers cannot and will not be answered!

Both common sense and propriety demand longer hair on a woman, no matter what she is doing. Her longer hair, as we have seen in verse 7, is her glory; it is her recognition of divine provision. This is her submission to God while she waits for Him to bring her to the companion man of His design at the right time under the right conditions. If the woman does not recognize God's AUTHORITY, she will never recognize the AUTHORITY of her companion man. Here is where her relationship to God and her relationship to her companion man meet. The woman who has negative volition (act of will) toward Bible doctrine, scar tissue (hardening of the heart) emotional revolt and reversionism does not have the capacity for LOVE. There are men that are intolerant of their wives/women attending Bible classes. But by "bucking the tiger" so to speak, they are destroying her capacity to develop deep (meat) understanding and are destroying their own AUTHORITY as a man. So Bible doctrine becomes important as the means of recognizing the principle of companion man – companion helper woman. Because of this danger, the next verse switches to the male. In effect, there are two witnesses against a man's having long hair – Bible doctrine and nature.

The Demonstration of Nature

1 Corinthians 11:14;
14 "Doesn't the nature of things itself teach you that a man who wears his hair long degrades himself?

or "does not even nature (in addition to Bible doctrine) communicate to all of you that if a man wears long hair, it is a dishonor to him?"

"**Nature**" means God's laws in the natural realm. Just as God has laws of establishment in the human realm, so God has laws with regard to nature. The term "nature" is really a misnomer (act of applying a wrong name). The Greek word **PHUSIS** refers to the laws of the function of nature within a species, which also vary within the species. Here we are talking about Homo sapiens – mankind. The fact that a woman with longer hair naturally looks like a woman and a man with short hair looks like a man is the principle which is being taught here.

But there is also another principle: in the animal kingdom, the male has the beauty; he has the mane or the ruff or the bright feathers. In Homo sapiens it is the opposite. The man was never designed to be beautiful! He can be attractive or even handsome, but it is the female who has the beauty. A lot of men are "fatheaded" about the way they look, but how a man looks does not mean a thing. It is how the woman looks that counts. Why? It is the woman who completes you, and her beauty is a part of it. I have seen a male who thought he was handsome (God's gift to women kind), who had the ability to love or to satisfy his companion helper woman, but, he is too busy primping and strutting like a peacock!

Both nature and Bible doctrine coincide in the area of companion man and companion helper woman. The differences in the male and the female body are nature's demonstration of this principle. Desires of soul and body are another testimony of nature. Now here is a third: long hair is out of place on the head of the man. Only under certain extreme circumstances, such as prolonged battlefield conditions, is long hair not a dishonor to man. If a man wears long hair – regardless of fashion, regardless of the period of history – it is always a dishonor to him. It is dishonorable because the man is wearing the woman's badge of submission! Long hair on a man is the result of the condition of his soul – scar tissue, emotional revolt and reversionism – just as extremely short hair is on a woman. Furthermore, it is a sign of a feminine soul in the man, as well as rebellion against God's design – against God's perfect divine law – and against the first grace gift ever given to the human race.

The Significance of Woman's Long Hair

1 Corinthians 11:15;
15 "But a woman who wears her hair long enhances her appearance, because her hair has been given to her as a covering."
or
But if a woman wears long hair, it is a glory to her, because her hair has been given to her instead of a veil (covering).

We now have a contrast between the short hair of the man and the longer hair of the woman. When a man wears long hair, it's a disgrace; but when a woman wears long hair, it is a veil of honor – a sign of her recognition of God's provision of a companion man. "IF," in both verses 14 and 15, is a third class condition and recognized the volition of both male and female. A woman can cut her hair just as a man can let his grow long.

"But if a woman wears long hair, it is a glory to her."

"TO HER" is an advantage. It is to her advantage to receive her companion man, to complete him. She fulfills him, as he fulfills her; and her long hair is not only beautiful, but it represents her positive volition (mind set / will) toward her companion man, her capacity to love, her freedom from mental attitudes of sin, scar tissue, emotional revolt, reversionism, and the perversions of reverse process reversionism.

"Her hair has been given" again emphasizes the first gift of Jesus Christ to the human race, and it is in the perfect tense, indicating the permanence of this principle. From the Garden of Eden to the end of the Millennium, the principle of the woman's long hair is always the same. It is the sign, just as the rainbow in the sky is a sign. The rainbow means that God will never again destroy the earth by flood, while the longer hair of the woman demonstrates that God has provided in every generation a companion man for a companion helper woman.

The next phrase is very important as it stands in the Greek text. The veil or covering is a literal veil, a hat, a bonnet, or anything that a woman might put on her head. However, it is not **"FOR A COVERING"** - BUT, **"INSTEAD OF A COVERING (OR A VEIL)."** And this is where the legalists have had it! Her **HAIR** has been given to her instead of a covering! God has never laid down any rules for women to wear hats! This has merely become a custom. (The cult of Traditionalism) Obviously there was a time when the wearing of veils was a good thing in many ways; but it was still unnecessary, according to God's standards. Every woman has been given glory by God, and even nature proves the point!

1 Corinthians 11:16;

16 "However, if anyone wants to argue about it, the fact remains that we have no such custom, nor do the Messianic communities of God.

But if anyone presumes to be contentious (rejecting authority), we have not this kind of a custom – neither the churches of God.

Of course, there are always rebels, as in verse 16, and they can be male or female. Those who have scar tissue or are in emotional revolt or reversionism and who reject authority, become contentious or quarrelsome. Paul puts them down by stating flatly that there is no such custom as wearing some kind of headgear in church. Thank God we have such a passage because of the erroneous idea that women must wear hats or veils in church! This has come from a misinterpretation of this passage or simply because ladies have been taught that a "proper lady" wears a hat in to worship. Hats are not desirable in worship for several reasons – visibility, concentration, and even the danger of mental attitude sins of competition with other women. The church is no place for anything but the glory of the Lord, and the glory of the Lord is overtly demonstrated in two ways in this passage: by man's short hair, in contrast to the woman's longer hair, and by the Communion Table.

Now our subject changes to a negative aspect as found in Proverbs 5, where we see the problem of pseudo-love.

Bible Doctrine, Guardian of the Soul and Body

It is my opinion that the man who translated Proverbs 5 was so sheltered he never saw a woman. When I get into the translation you will see why. I am sure that for some of you the literal translation of this passage will be a shock; but I have to tell you what's really here, and I am not going to pull any "punches" so to speak. It's the Word of God – and it is life; so we might as well be realistic and learn what God has for us here. It may save a greater shock for you later on.

Proverbs 5:1;

1 "My son, pay attention to my wisdom; incline your ear to my understanding ..."

"My son" indicates that Solomon has recorded the doctrine which his father, King David made a few mistakes himself, and of course he did not want Solomon to repeat them – although Solomon did repeat King David's mistakes a thousand times. Now, how are we going to learn? The ear is an organ of learning. To **"extend the ear"** means **"to accept my Father, King David's, AUTHORITY as a teacher."** The mother teaches the son up to a certain age; then the father must begin to teach things to the young man, as King David did to his son Solomon. The word for **"understanding"** refers to the application of Bible doctrine to the life – so **LEARN** and then **APPLY!**

Proverbs 5:2;
2 ".....so that you will preserve discretion and your lips keep watch over knowledge."
or
To guard against devisiveness; as for knowledge, that your lips may guard it.

"Divisiveness" is in the feminine gender; therefore, we know this is a warning to guard against the divisiveness of a reversionistic woman – the wrong woman, who can lure the man into fornication and ruin him for his companion helper woman. The thought is broken in the second half of the verse, and he goes back to Bible doctrine. There are two (2) different words for **"guard"** in this verse: **SHAMAR**, the first word, means **"to guard your soul."** The second word, **NATSAR**, is **"to guard physically, to guard your body."** Every man must guard his soul and his body and therefore preserve them for his companion helper woman. When you put the first two verses together, they tell us that every man must guard his soul and his body through **BIBLE DOCTRINE**. Taking in doctrine and learning its application is the greatest way to wait for the companion helper woman or the companion man.

King David – Bathsheba

The following is a small bit of history of King David and the culture of his day.
Boaz was a leading authority in the Torah of his day.

Israel men and women were not to marry a Moabite. The night that Boaz and Ruth married – Boaz supposedly died. But Ruth had conceived Obed. Obed was the father of Jesse, the father of King David. Ruth became the Grandmother of David.

1 Chronicles 2:12;
12 And Boaz begat Obed, and Obed begat Jesse,

    David was supposedly the illegitimate son of Jessee. This may or may not be incorrectly concluded or not logical. May or may not be a half-bother to the other 7 brothers – sons of Jesse... David was considered an embarrassment to the brothers. He had to eat his meals in a corner by himself. They put "gall" in his meal and gave him vinegar to drink to quench his thirst. He was also sent to the fields to tend the sheep as his brothers hoped he would be killed by a wild animal and they would be rid of him and the community embarrassment.
    David's Mother (with child) became evident, the husband, "Jesse" assumed it was the result of adultery as they had not had relations in years... (or so he thought)... there are two sides to this story. Jesse was to take a Canaanite maid servant and the maid servant had compassion on Jesse's wife and she told her the plan of Jesse and they supposedly switched places... Jesse was unaware of the switch. So it was assumed that his wife had had an adulterous affair. The sons wanted to stone her, and their father chose not to put her away, or have her stoned... they could not find a father...and he told his sons to leave her alone. We are not told which story is true... David's father was ½ and ½. Half Moabite and half Jew – remember Ruth was a Moabite.
    The community treated David as a treacherous sinner full of unspeakable guilt – shunned by town people, if something was lost or stolen, David was accused as the natural culprit and ordered in the words of the Psalm – to

"repay what I have not stolen."
David was a stranger to his brothers and a foreigner to his Mother's sons. His Mother grieved for years, she loved David with all her heart, but being his Mother put her in a position of not breaking Torah. She was required to be obedient to Jesse above all else earthly.

David's status was small in the eyes of Jesse -
David had red hair (shall shed blood)
David had a ruddy complexion (warlike appearance)
David had beautiful eyes (kindness)
David was handsome to look at.

Psalm 118:22 (David's Mother said)
Psalm 26:2
David was anointed King of Israel...
Sin is judged righteously as "measure for measure"...
Did David commit adultery – (No) according to Jewish culture/beliefs.
Did David murder – (No) according to a King's authority
    Clarification: The sages record that King David requested that all of his soldiers were required to give their wives a "GET" - a bill of divorcement before they went off to battle. This was done so that if the soldier failed to return from battle and his body was not found – the wife would not become an "ALGUNA" a woman who could not remarry. She could legally remarry if her husband did not return after a reasonable length of time. The "GET" was between "HIM and HER."

Leviticus 20:10; (Stoned)
10 And the man that committeth adultery with *another* man's wife, *even he* that committeth adultery with his neighbour's wife, the adulterer and the adulteress shall surely be put to death.

Bath-sheba was coming out of the "Mikveh" - the ritual bath and her exalter spiritual state attracted King David. He **PROPHETICALLY** saw that he was to father Solomon with this woman that was why he took her.

For though wash thee with "NITRE" and take thee much soap....

Jeremiah 2:22;
22 "Although you wash yourself with lye and use much soap, the stain of your iniquity is before me," declares the Lord God.

1. One sin before God leaves a mark.
2. The 2nd sin or the same sin before God is marked deepened.
3. The 3rd same sin becomes a stain spreading from 1 side to the other – as expressed – thy iniquity – it became a sin before me.

When David committed his "GREAT SIN" in taking Bathsheba, he thought it would leave its mark forever – but the message came to him: "The Lord hath put away thy sin, thou shall not die." But Nathan told David the following;

2 Samuel 12:13–15;
13 Then David said to Nathan, "I have sinned against the Lord." Nathan replied, "The Lord has taken away your sin. You are not going to die.
14 But because by doing this you have shown utter contempt for the Lord, the son born to you will die."
15 After Nathan had gone home, the Lord struck the child that Uriah's wife had borne to David, and he became ill.

"However, because by this deed you have given occasion to the enemies of the Lord to blaspheme, the child also that is born to you shall surely die." And Nathan went to his house.

Bath-Sheba was first Uriah's. Such is the way of the "Holy one" although a woman is destined for a certain man or men, he allows her to be the wife of another, until his time arrives.

As soon as his time arrives (death) he departs from the world to make room for another. He knows his (David) transgression and that's why Canaan (the Holy Land) was given to them before Israel.

Uriah disobeyed a "DIRECT ORDER" the first time, so King David gave him a second chance...

2 Samuel 11:10-12;
10 And when they had told David, saying, Uriah went not down unto his house, David said unto Uriah, Camest thou not from *thy* journey? why *then* didst thou not go down unto thine house?
11 And Uriah said unto David, The ark, and Israel, and Judah, abide in tents; and my lord Joab, and the servants of my lord, are encamped in the open fields; shall I then go into mine house, to eat and to drink, and to lie with my wife? *as* thou livest, and *as* thy soul liveth, I will not do this thing.
12 And David said to Uriah, Tarry here to day also, and to morrow I will let thee depart. So Uriah abode in Jerusalem that day, and the morrow.

Uriah disobeyed a direct order a second time. David had no choice; the penalty for disobedience is death.

2 Samuel 11:14-17;
14 And it came to pass in the morning, that David wrote a letter to Joab, and sent *it* by the hand of Uriah.
15 And he wrote in the letter, saying, Set ye Uriah in the forefront of the hottest battle, and retire ye from him, that he may be smitten, and die.
16 And it came to pass, when Joab observed the city, that he assigned Uriah unto a place where he knew that valiant men

were.
17 And the men of the city went out, and fought with Joab: and there fell *some* of the people of the servants of David; and Uriah the Hittite died also.

King David knows Uriah has an "EVIL HEART" never the less one must obey the King no matter what. David did not wish to publically shame Uriah, so David had him killed in battle in an honorable manner. Joab did not protest in the least because Joab knew the order of the King – as the Chief Justice.

What was David's Sin? More about this in the coming text.

2 Samuel 11:26;
26 So, Bath-sheba mourned the death of Uriah and then David took her as his appointed wife.

King David was also the Chief Judge. Nathan the Prophet came to the King for a judgment. 2 Samuel 12:13. The bottom line is: Hashem has accused King David of stealing a Ewe, a female sheep. Here is the penalty is therefore, in keeping with the sin.

Exodus 22:1;
1 If a man shall steal an ox, or a sheep, and kill it, or sell it; he shall restore five oxen for an ox, and four sheep for a sheep.

Evil: Every other evil and he did this evil. "To do" He did not. Uriah should have been tried by the Sanhedrin, but David did not!!!! Uriah was rebellious against royal authority – by saying - "My Lord Joab and servant are encamped in the open field."
So, we have:
    1. The sin of Uriah...
    2. The matter of Bath-Sheba

3. The counting of the people because King David was enticed.
4. David was punished...shall restore the sheep four (4) fold.
5. The child died.
6. Amnon
7. Tamar
8. Absalom

The sin of counting the people – King David was punished... a pestilence upon Israel from the morning even to the time appointed. King David's body was not punished for Uriah or Bath-Sheba.

King David was punished for 6 months as he was smitten with leprosy – the Sanhedrin was/is removed from him.... The Shekinah departed from Him...

Nevertheless, King David did sin grievously for a man in his exalted position with his exalted spiritual status. 2 Samuel 12:7-13. satan came to David in the shape of a "BIRD" when he looked upon Bath-Sheba and then "Flew as a bird to your mountain"... it was a dart slung at David's heart to not wait on the "HOLY ONE" to have Bath-Sheba in God's own time.

She belonged to David from the 6th day of creation. But he enjoyed her before she was ripe.

Psalm 51:2-5; (watch the punishment to see the sin.)
2 Wash away all my iniquity and cleanse me from my sin.
3 For I know my transgressions, and my sin is always before me.
4 Against you, you only, have I sinned and done what is evil in your sight; so you are right in your verdict and justified when you judge.
5 Surely I was sinful at birth, sinful from the time my mother conceived me.

Bath-Sheba became a Proverbs 31 woman. She was a

comfort, counterpart and completor to King David, she had his back...

The Divisive Woman

Proverbs 5:3;
3 "For the lips of a woman who is a stranger drop honey, her mouth is smoother than oil;"
or
for distilled honey (intoxicating sweetness) drips from the lips of her that is loathsome (reversionistic), and smoother (more flattering) than oil is the inside of her mouth.

Here is the description of the divisive or wrong woman. This kind of woman knows how to lead a man on. Her words are sweet droppings of honey dripping from the lips. She has a way with words that set him on fire. This is why he has to be alert in his soul. His soul has to be protected from this doll. There is one part of the woman's body that is always visible to the man under circumstances of intimacy, and that's her mouth. But the Hebrew word means **"the inside of the mouth."** Today we would call such intimacy the **"French kiss."** In other words, she has not talked very long before they were French-kissing! Her kisses were nice, but deceitful!

Proverbs 5:4;
4 "....but in the end she is as bitter as wormwood, sharp as a double-edged sword."

We are not filled in on all the details, but we understand that the intimacy ended in fornication. This is saying that the consequence of sex with her is the bitter curse of wormwood and does not bring blessings or life. Why is it bitter when it started out to be so much fun? She is not his companion helper woman! He is not her companion man. Wormwood is a poisonous plant found in Palestine. Although it has a bitter taste, it was used as a drug because it apparently had some kind of exhilarating effect. The users chewed it to get "high." Of course it was fun while it was being chewed, but it always left a terrible hangover. It poisoned the body!

The plant represents bitterness, sorrow and calamity.

Lamentations 3:15 & 19;
15 "He has filled me with bitterness, sated me with wormwood."
19 Remembering mine affliction and my misery, the wormwood and the gall.
Amos 5:7;
7 "You who turn justice to bitter wormwood and throw righteousness to the ground."

It is used in connection with reversionism in the practice of the phallic cult in Deuteronomy 29:18; Jeremiah 9:15; and 23:15.

Deuteronomy 29:18;
18 "....Let there not be among you a root earing such bitter poison and wormwood.
Jeremiah 9:15 & 23:15
15 ".....therefore." says ADONAI-TZVA'OT, the God of Israel: "I will feed the people bitter wormwood and give them poisonous water to drink."
23:15 Therefore, this is what ADONAI-TZVA'OT says concerning the prophets: "I will feed them bitter wormwood and make them drink poisonous water, for ungodliness has spread through all the land from the prophets of Yerushalayim." (Jerusalem).

In other words, the affair has a bitter ending. King David is saying to Solomon, **"Wait, wait, wait, boy!"** Solomon says, **"Sure, sure, Dad!"** And he goes right out and gets involved with many wrong women – reversionistic women (1 Kings 11:1-8). Vs. 1 "King Solomon loved many foreign women besides the daughter of Pharoah. There were women from the Mo'avi, 'Amoni, Edomi, Tzidoni and Hitti –Vs. 2 nations about which ADONAI had said to the people of Israel.

1 Kings 11:2;
2 Of the nations *concerning* which the LORD said unto the children of Israel, Ye shall not go in to them, neither shall they come in unto you: *for* surely they will turn away your heart after their gods: Solomon clave unto these in love.

But Solomon was deeply attached to them by his love. Vs. 3 - He had 700 wives, all princesses, and 300 concubines; and his wives turned his heart away. Vs. 4 – For when Solomon became old, his wives turned his heart away toward other gods; so that he was not wholehearted with ADONAI his God, as David his father had been. Vs. 5 – For Solomon followed 'Ashtoret the goddess of the Tzidoni and Mjilkom the abomination of the 'Amoni. Vs. 6 – Thus Solomon did what was evil in ADONAI'S view and did not fully follow ADONAI, as David his father had done. Vs. 7 – Solomon built a high place for K'mosh the abomination of Mo'av on the hill in front of Yerushalayim, and another for Molekh the abomination of he people of 'Amon. Vs. 8 – This is what he did for all his foreign wives, who then offered and sacrificed to their gods."........

Solomon's Mother gave him instruction in Proverbs 31 about a wonderful wife and we know of course that he did not listen to his Father, David or his Mother, Bathsheba.

This type of woman is an inconsequential person to a man. He should be waiting for someone wonderful. And to the extent that he fools around this way, it will be bitter, bitter, bitter! It may destroy his capacity for companion helper woman and vice versa. Let's remember, this is always a two-way street. When the wrong woman or the wrong man gets his hooks into you – whether you are male or female, it is like being stabbed with a very short sword; it is like being poisoned!

Pathway to Destruction

Proverbs 5:5;
5 "Her feet go down to death, her steps lead straight to Sh'ol" Her seductive feet are going down to death; her sexy, mincing steps embrace the grave.

This woman has just wrecked a man; now we follow her down the pathway to destruction. The ladies in the ancient world did not display as much of the body as do women in our day. Their heads and their feet were about all that were visible. I dare to say that few men today are turned on by a woman's feet. But in those days a woman's feet were one of her methods of seduction, and her feet – used for seduction – are going down to death. **MEWETH, MAWETH** is derived from a Hebrew verb which means **"to stretch like a corpse."** This is a description of the sin unto death. She is not going to hell, as it says in the English. **"My son"** is a believer, the woman is a believer. This will head off at the pass those of us who think that promiscuity is practiced only by unbelievers.

"Her steps" connotes a sexy walk as a **"come-on."** These women usually wore ornamental ankle chains and tiny bells to call attention to their sexy steps. But get this: her sexy walk **EMBRACES THE GRAVE.** Every time she embraces a man who is not her companion man, every time she fornicates, she is taking another step toward getting in bed with the grave. That's actually what it is saying. It is very humorous! She prides herself on how great she is on her back, so she is going to wind up on her back – IN A WOODEN BOX!!!! No woman can afford promiscuity, nor can a man. God has designed something wonderful for those who wait. Those who do not wait lose something wonderful. Even if they find their companion man or companion helper woman, they have a difficult time. Their reputation breeds suspicion, and it produces mental attitude sins.

This passage is particularly applicable to you single people who are still waiting. Just keep on waiting! No one ever gains by fornicating around. After all, you are waiting for something that's the concentrated essence of human happiness. You are waiting for something that God provided for you in eternity past, as far back as Genesis 1:26. "Then God said,""Let us make humankind in our image, in the likeness of ourselves......."

Perhaps you should consider her manner of lives (instability and unfaithfulness); her manner of life wavers back and forth – you do not know her.

Proverbs 5:6;
6 Lest thou shouldest ponder the path of life, her ways are moveable, *that* thou canst not know *them*.

She doesn't walk the level path of life... her course wanders all over, but she doesn't know it.

"Perhaps," David continues to warn Solomon, "you should take some academic advice while you still have a chance – you should consider her manner of lives. Before you get taken in by this beautiful, attractive, seductive doll, you had better remember that she has had many lovers, many acts of social, mental, and sexual unfaithfulness. She's gone to bed with fifty men, and you are fifty-one! What makes you think that you are so special? You are not her companion man; you are just another victim, another sucker. You are another 'wormwood' in the making, and she is another step closer to an affair with the grave. You just help her along!

"Her manner of life is a dead end. She's full of scar tissue. She has no capacity to love you. She will say all the right words to turn you on; but she has you so fooled and faked out that you think you are the greatest thing in the world. But you do not understand her. She is already looking past you to the next conquest." Now you see where the father's teaching becomes necessary. The mother brings in respect for womanhood. Then the father tempers it with his wisdom.

Listen to me now sons, and do not depart (deviate) from the words of my mouth.

Proverbs 5:7;
7 Hear me now therefore, O ye children, and depart not from the words of my mouth.

Although David is speaking to his sons, it is also the Holy Spirit speaking through David to all believers (2 Samuel 23:2). And I want you to remember that as we get into this next section. God the Holy Spirit has seen fit to enlighten us with regard to the first great grace gift and He has done so in very plain and lucid language. If you tend toward prudishness of asceticism and this is too personal, YOU are out of line! Every jot and tidle of the Word of God is the THINKING OF JESUS CHRIST and do not forget it!

Sex between companion man and the companion helper woman is a grace gift from Jesus Christ. There is nothing bad about it, it is good! It is great! There was never a grace gift that was wrong or bad or that must be treated in a hush-hush manner. The first grace gift had to come in order for a greater grace gift to come. The incarnation of Jesus Christ could not occur until we have woman, who gives birth to children and has all the accouterments for it! I want you to understand that we are dealing with the Word of God; we are dealing with doctrine and with grace principles. There's just as much grace in sex as there is in the food on your table. Have you ever said grace over sex!

Avoid Temptation – WOW!!

Get you way of life far away from over above her, and do not come near the door of her house.

Proverbs 5:8;
8 Remove thy way far from her, and come not nigh the door of her house:

Distance your way from her, stay far from the door of her house ..."
"From over above her" is one of the ways of describing the sex act. In other words, remove your sex life from her vicinity! Do not even approach the door of her house. Why not?
Lest you give your glory (sex) to the pseudos, and your years (of sexual vigor) to the cruel or vindictive (reversionistic woman).

Proverbs 5:9;
9 Lest thou give thine honour unto others, and thy years unto the cruel:

David is anxious for his sons to wait for their right women. Each will face temptations which will cause them to deviate from this principle. It is important that they stay on the main track. Otherwise, sex becomes an idol, as we will see in verses 21 and 22, and every affair is a chain or a cord binding them to this idol. Verse 9 begins with the word "lest" to head you off at the pass – a warning to avoid an affair with the wrong woman while it is still only a temptation.

Proverbs 6:20-22;
20 My son, keep thy father's commandment, and forsake not the law of thy mother:
21 Bind them continually upon thine heart, *and* tie them about thy neck.
22 When thou goest, it shall lead thee; when thou sleepest, it shall keep thee; and *when* thou awakest, it shall talk with thee.

Whenever you find "glory" in Scripture, it is something

that belongs to God and that God shares only through grace. You never earn it. "Glory" here is man's ability to fulfill a woman sexually. But watch it – ONE WOMAN! The glory of the man is his COMPANION HELPER WOMAN. When he provides sex for his companion helper woman, she lights up like a Hanakkuh light. She is glorious! The companion helper woman is designed to be insatiable, and her companion man is the only person who has the key to her lock; he is the only person who has the ability to satisfy and fulfill her – soul and body. Every time a man gets in bed with a wrong woman, he has given his glory to someone else – not to his companion woman. Now you may think that you are a sex athlete and God's gift to women, and that you have enough glory to pass around to every woman in the world! If you do, God's Word says you have had it. Now listen, men, your glory, your sex – all of it – belongs to one woman – not to several, not to a boy or another man, not to an animal, and not to yourself! One woman!

Time is usually measured in days, but time wasted in fornication is called "years". When you give your glory to a reversionistic woman, this type of woman is vindictive and will take the glory and turn to bitterness. This is known as "a boomerang." But when you give your glory to the companion helper woman, she REFLECTS your glory.

The Consequences of Promiscuity

Lest promiscuous women become satiated with your vigor, and your earthen vessel shattered in a whorehouse.

Proverbs 5:10;
10 Lest strangers be filled with thy wealth; and thy labours *be* in the house of a stranger;

And you groan in distress at your end, when your flesh (body) and your phallus are ruined.

Proverbs 5:11;
11 And thou mourn at the last, when thy flesh and thy body are consumed,

    The word translated "strangers" in your English Bible is a word we are going to see frequently throughout the rest of the passage. The stranger here is a woman who is promiscuous, who is a chippie or a whore, or who is just "free and easy." Remember, the woman is insatiable; and when an insatiable woman latches on to the wrong man, he is squandering his wealth or vigor by satiating a promiscuous woman. This has to do with sexual performance. It can be translated academically, "Lest" adulteresses be satiated with your sex performance."

    This section is emphasizing the male, but the "vessel" can refer to either the male or female body. The man who gives his body to a whore has shattered it for his companion helper woman, and vice versa. He kept taking his earthen vessel – his human body – to a whorehouse or its equivalent, until finally one day it had wasted away. And what does he do? He groans in distress when his body functions fail. For the male, the end result of fornication is frustration, unhappiness and finally, impotence. The female either becomes a nymphomaniac and is totally indiscriminate, or she becomes completely and totally frustrated to the point that she is regarded as sexless. Both the general health and the genital system are adversely affected by sex with the wrong man or wrong woman. Then you (groan), Eck, I have hated disciplinary warning, and my right lobe despised and ridiculed corrective punishment

Proverbs 5:12;
12 And say, How have I hated instruction, and my heart despised reproof;

    Now we get to the death cry of the rogue. He cries,

"Eeeek!" That is the screeching of the brakes as the whole gear box falls apart. It is like the final wailing trumpet of the bull elephant as he leaves the herd and goes off alone to die. Now the rogue had a warning or two, but he refused to listen. He rejected discipline and authority under the principle of the laws of divine establishment. And here is a young man whose parental warnings not only went unheeded but were ridiculed.

And I have not listened and obeyed the voice of my instructors, nor concentrated on the message of those who have taught me.

Proverbs 5:13;
13 And have not obeyed the voice of my teachers, nor inclined mine ear to them that instructed me!

Connecting this with the foregoing verses, the point he is making is that if people would use the organ of perception, they would use the organ of sex to better advantage. But Solomon, who wrote this after it had been fulfilled, admittedly failed.

Shortly I was in all evil in both the worship assembly and in the function of the nation.

Proverbs 5:14;
14 "I took part in almost every kind of evil, and the whole community knew it."

In "kind of evil" refers to his reversionism plus the practice of reverse process reversionism in love – hence, Solomon's promiscuity. Why was he in this situation? Because he had refused to listen his Mother Bathsheba and the worship assembly, as well as to the instruction of his own Father. Negative volition toward doctrine led to scar tissue, emotional revolt and reversionism. This, in turn, led to the rejection of the principle of companion man – companion helper woman. The inevitable result was fornication and promiscuity. As far as the function of the nation was concerned, Solomon was the king, and it is difficult for a people to rise above the failure and apostasy of its leadership,

The rest of this chapter is vitally important to the doctrine of companion man – companion helper woman; yet it is so poorly translated and so obscured by anachronism (refers to a wrong time) that it is almost impossible for anyone to derive the intended blessing from this passage as it stand in the Authorized Version. It is intended not only to emphasize the first of the three great gifts from God the Son - companion man – companion helper woman – but also to ward off its many dangers and enemies. The fact that God has designed one right man for one right woman does not guarantee automatic happiness or that everyone will find his right woman or right man. Therefore, in verse 15 - "Drink the water from your own cistern, fresh water from your own well." we have an analogy which is always used in connection with grace gifts.

The Prohibition of Adultery

Drink waters of pleasure from your own cistern, and flowing waters from your own well

Proverbs 5:15;
15 Drink waters out of thine own cistern, and running waters out of thine own well.

First of all, there is a command to drink water. Water, as an analogy of grace, is used three ways in the Word of God. Here, water is the COMPANION HELPER WOMAN. Water in Isaiah 55:1 is SALVATION. Water in Ephesians 5:26 is DOCTRINE. And once again we have the three great grace gifts from God to man. The command to drink indicates that all grace gifts must be received. However, this word literally means "to drink and enjoy it" or "to drink and have your thirst quenched." It has a meaning of living it up in a good sense. In this context, it is used for the man who is sexually thirsty for his companion helper woman. His thirst is quenched, and he is gratified in his relationship with her. This is one of the greatest happiness's of life. All of the great happiness's of life are related to the gifts of grace.

"Water of pleasure" is plural because there are many acts of sexual relationship between right man and right woman. But please notice; "from your OWN WELL." There are many acts of "drinking" but one well – right woman. A cistern, in Hebrew phraseology, refers to a covered well – Cf.

2 Kings 18:31;
31 Hearken not to Hezekiah: for thus saith the king of Assyria, Make *an agreement* with me by a present, and come out to me, and *then* eat ye every man of his own vine, and every one of his fig tree, and drink ye every one the waters of his cistern: (flowing water).

The companion helper woman is covered to everyone else. Who pulls the cover off the well? Only the companion man. She is designed to be appreciated by one man only. Therefore, the companion helper woman should be discreet in her dress. You can always tell a woman who isn't a right woman – she's advertising! A right woman who is satisfied is not concerned with displaying herself; and while she dresses as tastefully as possible, obviously she does not try to attract other men with her dress. A woman who is flirty, who wears her clothing a little too short or cut a little too low, is obviously not a "cistern". She is on the prowl, and she is easily detected by those with doctrine or discernment.

The second analogy, "flowing waters," represents the same principle. However, this time, since the waters are running, the well is not covered. So we have a different Hebrew word. The first word indicates the outside – the well is covered. But where the companion man is, the well is NOT COVERED. The "flowing waters" describe the sex response of a woman to her companion man. "Flowing: has another beautiful connotation. When you are in the water, it always accommodates itself perfectly to your body. That's the key here. In divine design there is a perfect physical coalescence (the state of being united – growing together). Divine design program and the companion helper woman for the companion man only. Therefore, ADULTERY IS PROHIBITED. If either man or woman fornicates under reverse process reversionism, they destroy their programming.

    A third analogy from this verse is that as the waters flow to slake the thirst of man, so the sexual response of the woman gives complete satisfaction. Nothing really quenches the thirst like plain, cool water; and no matter how plain a woman may appear overtly, she was designed by God to satisfy the thirst of one man. Once again, David is trying to teach Solomon: wait for your companion helper woman; she is the only one who can slake your thirst!

    A fourth analogy is that when anyone swallows cool or cold water, the body heat immediately takes care of it. By the time it reaches the stomach, it is warmer than it was before; it adjusts itself to the body temperature. Just so, in the relationship between companion man and companion helper woman, the woman is also satisfied; however, the danger is that if she enters into fornication or adultery, she becomes dissatisfied and frustrated. In her frustration, she is willing to give herself to anyone in the hope that just around the corner there will be some man who will satisfy her physically. She is trying to find divine design, but she's going about it in the wrong way. It's like the water jumping out of the well and splashing itself on every stranger who walks by. Well is not designed to do that. The water waits in the well for the one who has a right to drink there. If the water is all splashed out through fornication by the time the right one comes along, there is nothing in the well but sand; and I have never seen anyone yet who was satisfied with a bucket of sand when he wanted water!

There is a further analogy of this principle in Song of Solomon 4:12: "A garden enclosed is my sister, my spouse; a spring shut up, a fountain sealed." The "fountain sealed: is a virgin. Here is a woman who is holding all of her water for the quenching thirst of the companion man. In these days of apostasy, we have the new sex movement in which you are supposed to experiment or shop around until you find what you want. But the Word of God teaches that this destroys the programming for companion man – companion helper woman, and that the greatest relationship between companion man and companion helper woman comes when both of them have waited. This eliminates hang-ups and problems, and their relationship becomes a very beautiful thing.

Another verse, which is closely related to the analogy in Proverbs 5:15, is found in Proverbs 23:26: "For a whore is a deep ditch; and a strange woman is a narrow pit." It is impossible to get water out of a deep ditch; therefore, the person who goes to the deep ditch or the narrow pit for the alleviation of thirst never succeeds. In other words, a person who goes to a whore to satisfy his libido is not going to have his soul-thirst satisfied. The water cannot be reached.

It is also dangerous to drink from open ditches. The water was polluted. Therefore, not only does one not receive the quenching of thirst from the deep ditch, but one might pick up disease. By analogy, of course, this would be venereal disease. It was safe to drink only from your own cistern, which was a covered storage for rainwater, or to drink running water, which was pure. Even though a man and a woman thrown together under the circumstances of prostitution might have been programmed for each other, reverse process reversionism renders them incapable of knowing this. The whore has made what water she had for her companion man unavailable to him, and he has spent so much time exploiting sex, they simply become "ships that pass in the night." Both of them, have destroyed that wonderful thing which is one of the greatest happiness's in life. When God forbids adultery, He's not being unkind. He's trying to save something that is really great for every one of you!

"Thine own well" means the companion helper woman that God has designed for you only. Every time you go to another well, you are trying to make it your own. You are trying to program that well to you – to manufacture your companion helper woman out of everyone with whom you fornicate. You will never slake your thirst at anyone else's well. Many a man goes through life being totally frustrated because he's drinking at everyone else's well.

Proverbs 9:17-18;
17 Stolen waters are sweet, and bread *eaten* in secret is pleasant.
18 But he knoweth not that the dead *are* there; *and that* her guests *are* in the depths of hell.

Remember, like the other grace gifts, sex must be understood within the framework of divine design. The One who designed these things for our happiness also set up some laws and boundaries. The laws of divine establishment contain laws for sex. This is what is being brought out.

The "well of water" which belongs to you must be regarded as one of the highest things on your scale of values. In the Biblical scale of values, number one is salvation, then Bible doctrine, and third, companion man or companion helper woman. Anyone who finds his companion helper woman must consider himself extremely wealthy.

Proverbs 31:10;
10 Who can find a capable wife? Her value is far beyond that of pearls."

There are possessions more important than money, and this is one of them.

While people in the ancient world knew very little about money or attached little importance to it, one thing was valued above all else, and that was the well.

John 4:12;
12 "You aren't greater than our father Ya'akov (Jacob), are you? He gave us this well and drank from it, and so did his sons and his cattle."

When moving or traveling, the Jews always stopped by a well. They lived by a well. There is a sense in which a companion man must live by the well – his companion helper woman. She should be more important to him than anything or anyone else in the world, with the exception of salvation and doctrine.

The Man's Aggressiveness

Your fountains shall not overflow (to other women), in the streets a dividing of the waters.

Proverbs 5:16;
16 "Let what your springs produce be dispersed outside, streams of water flowing in the streets ..."

I want you to notice a change from the previous verse. There the water referred to the woman. But in this verse the fountains are gushing waters and are a picture of the male sex drive. In the well and in the cistern the water lies placid, what does it do in a fountain? It bubbles up and down, up and down. The water becomes very turbulent, and this indicates the companion helper woman's extreme, beautiful, glorious passion. What stirs it up? A fountain – the force of water. It is the man who is thirsty; it is the woman who is stirred up. How does the man relieve his thirst? By drinking from the well. That means the woman satisfies the man. How is she satisfied? By the sexual ability of the male to elicit response from his companion helper woman. In other words, no woman is placid when her companion man is making love to her. She is a storm of passion!

"Your fountain (sex with your companion helper woman) shall not overflow" - that is, to others. This is a prohibition of adultery or fornication, or even homosexuality. When a man's fountain, designed for his companion helper woman, overflows to others and the male sex aggressiveness goes into fornication, then it divides into streets. "Streets" refer to social life. Any group or organization is destroyed when there is a sharing of one well. There is social confusion. The higher the adultery index in a national entity, the more confusion there is. A nation of fornicators is a nation divided. They will never be able to get together to defend their nation or anything else.

"Let them (your sex acts) be for your one and only, and not for a reversionistic, promiscuous woman."

Proverbs 5:17;
17 Let them be only thine own, and not strangers' with thee.

Every time a man fornicates, he sells his birthright of wonderful happiness with his companion helper woman for a mess of pottage. What's more, he has tampered with God's design. No one-night stand with some attractive female is ever going to do anything but destroy.

Proverbs 6:32;
32 *But* whoso committeth adultery with a woman lacketh understanding: he *that* doeth it destroyeth his own soul.

Only her companion man is programmed to satisfy her physically and to quench the thirst of her soul at the same time, resulting in happiness so beautiful that only those who have been there can really understand it.

The Blessing of Companion Man – Companion Helper Relationship

Proverbs 5:18;
18 "Your fountain shall be permanently blessed; therefore, take pleasure in the woman of your vigor."

Find joy in her. "Fountain" refers again to the sexual aggressiveness of the companion man toward his companion helper woman. The next two verbs form a periphrastic (a method of speech) to emphasize the permanence of happiness in the relationship of companion man – companion helper woman, even under adverse circumstances. This verse must be regarded in the light of the previous verse. Your sex life will be blessed only when you take pleasure in the COMPANION HELPER WOMAN of your sexual vigor. The companion helper woman is described in the next verse.

"An amorous, sexy doe (symmetry conforms perfectly to companion man's body), a wild she-goat of grace. Her breasts shall intoxicate you at all times; you shall always wander (up and down her body) in the area of her love."

Proverbs 5:19;
19 "....a lovely deer, a graceful fawn; let her breasts satisfy you at all times, always be infatuated with her love."

The doe was known in Palestine for its symmetry and beauty. Therefore, the doe represents the symmetry and the beauty of the companion helper woman as the companion man sees her. As he observes her beauty and symmetry, he is aroused to many acts of love. The next description, "a pleasant roe," is a female goat or ibex - "a wild she-goat." This does not sound romantic to us. But the ancients observed that the wild she-goat was very expressive during the sex act and therefore was apparently quite satisfied. The word for "pleasant" is literally "grace" - a wild she-goat of grace. This indicates her magnificent wild passion in response to her companion man sexually. What is even more interesting is that the word for she-goat, JAALAH, has as its root a verb JAEL, which means "to help, to profit, to benefit." (to be a comfort, a counterpart, and a completor). This is the same concept we saw in Genesis 2. The companion helper woman is a help, benefit and profit to the companion man. Therefore, the wild she-goat of grace connotes the benefit of grace. Again this emphasizes the three grace gifts from Jesus Christ.

We now come to her breasts. This is one of those rather strange words in the Hebrew – a double D – that's all. To pronounce it, you have to put in a vowel, so you have "DAD." So this letter "D" in the dual form, plus the vowel, means the woman's breasts. The word translated "satisfy" is RAWAH, which has several meanings; but here it means "to be intoxicated with." "Her breasts shall intoxicate you at all times." The woman's breasts represent her sexual response.

The last phrase, "you will always wander up and down her body in the area of her love, "brings out the principle that anything to which both companion man and companion helper woman agree is permissible. There is no such thing as perversion in anything they do in their sex life together and to which both agree. But make sure it's your companion helper woman!

"And why, my son, should you wander up and down the body of a promiscuous woman, and embrace the genitals of a nymphomaniac?"

Proverbs 5:20;
20 "My son, why be infatuated with an unknown woman? Why embrace the body of a loose woman?"

Now the question is verse 20 indicates that David knew Solomon had a wandering, roving spirit; and although at the much later time, Solomon recorded it under the ministry of the Holy Spirit; he did not heed these words. He really blew it. The end of this verse is a prophecy about what happened to Solomon, as is the last phrase in the chapter, "the greatness of his folly." Solomon's failure reached a magnitude the like of which very few people have ever had the opportunity to experience. Solomon had one thousand affairs – seven hundred wives and three hundred concubines. Out of all of these, not one of them was his companion helper woman!

The Perfect Balance

Proverbs 5:21;
21 "For before the eyes of the Lord, the ways of man; he weighs all man's tracks."
Or
"For ADONAI is watching a man's ways; he surveys all his paths."

"The ways of man" refers to the pattern and function of life, described by the context as sex with the wrong woman. This is a man who has violated the laws of divine establishment and rejected the principle of companion man – companion helper woman. In his own way, by means of his sexual prowess, he seeks to remold and to remake the laws of establishment. Such a man is blasphemous! He is saying in effect, "God designed one woman for me, but I do not accept that, I can take any woman and reprogram her to respond to me."

Now the Lord knew everything about every man, and He knew it billions of years ago. The word translated "ponder" in the English actually means "to weigh in a balanced scale." The Lord weighs all of man's tracks – every act of fornication with the wrong man or wrong woman. God designed companion man and companion helper woman to be a perfect balance. When that balance is achieved, each provides great human happiness for the other. The man fulfills the woman, and the woman completes the man. However, when one or the other fornicates, the scales are tipped. The man who has spent his adult life experimenting with the female of the species of practicing any form of perversion does not bring to his companion woman all of himself, so they do not balance, and they do not derive the pleasure they otherwise would. In fact, that's one way God puts them on an even scale, but when they do things that upset the balance, they must reap what they sow. God does not actually discipline them right then and there. His judgment is simply allowing the inevitable consequences o take effect – unhappiness and self-induced misery.

The Slavery of Promiscuity

Proverbs 5:22;
22 "A wicked person's own crimes will trap him, he will be held fast by the ropes of his sin."
Or
"His own perversions will trap him with a reversionistic woman, and he shall be seized & bound with the chains (ropes) of his own feminine idol."

Anything that rejects the grace gift is a deviation from the norm and therefore perversion. The norm is the principle of companion man – companion helper woman. The perversion of this principle as we have seen, is fourfold; adultery or fornication, homosexuality or lesbianism, autoerotism and bestiality. A man's own perversions become a trap. Here is the balancing of the scale of divine judgment. When a reversionistic (being turned in an opposite direction) male fornicates with a reversionistic female, the scales of judgment are balanced instead of the scales of happiness. These two make each other miserable. They frustrate each other with their sex.

He is not only trapped, but notice, "He shall be bound with the chains of his own feminine idol." The reversionistic male is binding himself to an idol which he has created with his phallus. The idol of man's adulterous creation is not the companion helper woman created by God! Why is sex said to be an idol? Man, in fornication, has intruded upon God's grace and upon God's design. Man can create neither God nor God's design. What can man make and call it "GOD"? An idol. Paul said in 1 Corinthians 8:4, "We know that an idol is nothing." Proverbs 5 says that promiscuous or adulterous man ends up with nothing. You can make love to an idol, but an idol will never satisfy you. Every sexual conquest is one more chain binding you to the idol of sex. Even if you find and marry your companion helper woman, every time you get in bed with her, there are actually three people in bed – your idol, yourself and your companion helper woman.

There is another danger. The man who has been promiscuous often winds up marrying the wrong person. He is tied, bound, chained – and that's it. Along comes companion helper woman – but he's had it! Now, maybe you are thinking, "I can cut the ropes." But the Word of God says you CAN NOT cut the ropes. The fact that you are chained to the wrong one does not give you the right to jump out of marriage. So, if you thought you saw daylight, the door has just been slammed in your face! There are other doctrinal principles which can counteract your sins and failures – taking in doctrine under the daily function of "GAP," erecting an edification complex and moving into super-grace.

Proverbs 5:23;
23 "He will die from lack of discipline; the magnitude of his folly will make him totter and fall."
Or
"He shall die without doctrine, and in the magnitude of his folly, he shall go astray."

"Death" here is physical death. It means that the promiscuous man dies without doctrine. The believer who misses both doctrine and companion man or companion helper woman because of reversionism is a "one-third believer." He has lost two of the grace gifts. The only grace gift he cannot lost, of course is salvation and eternal life (that two is questionable without reading and studying and obeying Torah). The "abundance (for magnitude) of his folly" refers to the whole realm of failure in reversionism: negative volition toward doctrine, scar tissue of the soul, emotional revolt and the practice of reverse process reversionism. These destroy the capacity for love, because capacity is in the soul. This man shall go astray – literally, "he shall wander up and down." This time it does not mean to wander up and down the woman's body, but to wander up and down in life and never find the companion helper woman – an Adam without his spine!

For you who are still in single bliss, the state of being single has a serious responsibility. Do not make a mistake! Get the right one the FIRST time. Now, although companion helper woman was the initial gift, the other two, salvation and doctrine, give WISDOM, ASSURANCE AND STABILITY in finding and maintaining the first gift. While you are waiting, therefore, I cannot stress too often – KEEP TAKING IN DOCTRINE! Doctrine will protect you from disappointments and mistakes. Then at the right time God will bring along the companion helper woman and you will know her!!!

The Bride of Christ

When Jesus Christ looked at Adam before the woman was "built," He said, "LO TOBH" - "not good that man should be alone." So Jesus Christ provided a companion helper woman – a partner – for the first Adam. Grace takes care of aloneness, and a gracious gift was provided. The companion helper woman canceled out "LO TOBH."

Now it was good that Jesus Christ should be alone on the Tree (Cross); but just as man had to be alone after he was created so that the grace gifts could come, so the Last Adam had to be alone so that the gift of salvation could come to mankind. While bearing out sins on the Tree (Cross), God the Father and God the Holy Spirit forsook Jesus Christ (Matthew 27:46). When Christ came out from the grave, He was alone in resurrection body. Today Christ is seated at the right hand of the Father ALONE. He is waiting for a Bride. As Christ gave Adam a companion helper woman, so the Father gave the Son a "BRIDE woman" - the Church. The Bride, which is being prepared during the Church Age, is called a "Body" because it is being BUILT (Eph. 4:16). - " Under his control, the whole body is being fitted and held together by the support of every joint, with each part working to fulfill its function; this is how the body grows and builds itself up in love."

The rib is comparable to positional truth: believers are IN CHRIST as the rib (column, for stands upright) was in Adam. The rib was passionately pulled out to be made into a bride for Adam. At the Rapture, the Church will be caught up from the earth (1 Thess. 4:16-17), and the Body will become the Bride of Christ. The Father will present to the Son – the Last Adam – the Bride, the Body of Christ, just as Jesus Christ brought the woman to the first Adam. The Rapture is the presentation of the Bride in perfect resurrection body, without the old sin nature and without human good (Eph. 5:27) "...in order to present the Messianic Community to himself as a bride to be proud of, without a spot, wrinkle or any such thing, but holy and without defect."

Everything we have as believers is based on our relationship with the Lord, and many illustrations of our relationship with Him are taken from the principle of love. This is brought out every time the Church is described as the Bride with Jesus Christ as the Groom. In our relationship with the Lord, He is our Companion Man, and we as believers are His "Companion Helper woman" (Eph. 5:22-23). We have walked into a permanent love relationship with the Godhead. There never was a time when they did not love each other, when they did not have perfect capacity for each other. Jesus Christ took on the form of man so that we could have that perfect relationship with the Godhead. He provided eternal salvation, capacity to love Him, and every other benefit and blessing in life. But the realization of these blessings comes only through the knowledge of doctrine – Jesus Christ – as your Companion Man – initiates and expresses His love for you in His Word. Do you respond to Him?

A Heart like Jesus

Once, before the foundation of the world, Jesus and His Father had a conversation about the great plan of redemption.
THAT CONVERSATION INCLUDED YOU.
Jesus looked down the corridors of time and knew that YOU would be born.
He saw your needs when He said to His Father, "I will go."
AT THE FATHER'S APPOINTED TIME, Jesus came to earth so that you would never need to be far from Him.
What an incredible journey He made, what an overwhelming expression of LOVE He made, what an awesome purpose He had in mind.
YOU WERE ON HIS HEART.
When He left His home in heaven, He saw you; when He became a man on earth, He was SEEKING you; when He stretched out His hands upon the tree (cross), He was REACHING OUT to you, when He returned to His Father; He was and is preparing a place for you.
YOU ARE THE SHEEP He has come to SHEPHERD, to GUIDE, to FEED, to PROTECT, to SHELTER, and to CARRY.
You are the one He calls HIS OWN.
"…..'I have loved you with an everlasting love...'" Jeremiah 31:3

He came because He loves those whom the Father loves – He related with warmth and compassion to the Lower, Middle, and Upper Class not because of Financial clout, intelligence or social status, but because we are God's children. He came to the Poor, the Blind, the Lepers, the Hungry Sinners, the Prostitutes, the Tax Collectors, the Persecuted, the Downtrodden, the Captives, those possessed by unclean spirits, all who labor and are heavy burdened, the ones who knew nothing of laws, the crowds, the little ones, the least, the last – Lost Sheep of the house of Israel and all others because He loves.

Listening to God is a firsthand experience. When He asks for your attention, God does not want you to send a substitute, HE WANTS YOU. He invites you to vacation in His splendor. He invites you to feel the touch of His hand. He invites you to feast at His table – the table of His word. He wants to spent time with you. Your time with God can be the highlight of your day. "But the Helper (Holy Spirit) will teach you everything and will cause you to remember all that I told you. This Helper is the Holy Spirit whom the Father will send in my name" - John 14:26. Jesus said: "Search and you will find" - Matthew 7:7 and "chew on Scripture day and night" - Psalm 1:2. The Bible is not a newspaper to be skimmed but rather a mine to be quarried. "Search for it like silver, and hunt for it like hidden treasure. Then you will understand respect for the Lord, and you will find that you know God." Proverbs 2:4-5.

Be like a child – un-self conscious and incapable of pretense.

7 Feast of the LORD Being Symbolic of New Life

Below is an overview of how the festivals of our Heavenly Father is liken unto new life.

Feast	Christian Fulfillment	Baby Development
Passover (Pesach) Fertilization must take place within 24 hours.	**New Life (Egg)** Leviticus 23:5	**Ovulation**
Unleavened Bread Matzoh Bread is stripped	**The Seed (Planting)** 1 Corinthians 5:7-8 Leviticus 23:6-8	**Fertilization** Christ buried
First Fruits Spring planting Leviticus 23:10-11; (Matthew 27:27-53; Early crop of believers)	**Resurrection** Resurrection Day Resurrection of the entire church	**Raised from dead**
Pentecost Acts 2:1-50 days from Reed Sea. 50 days Embryo becomes a fetus. Pentecost Greek word means 50.	**Harvest**	**New Creature** Fetus Sweet Holy Spirit

The 4 feast (festivals) above have been fulfilled at Pentecost. Christ breathed the Holy Spirit upon the disciples.

The following 3 festivals are unfulfilled. We await their fulfillment.

Feast	Christian Fulfillment	Baby Development
Trumpets 1st day of 7th month the baby can hear.	**Catching Up (Rapture)** Joshua 6:5 1 Thessalonians 4:16-17	**Hearing**

Feast	Christian Fulfillment	Baby Development
Day of Atonement 10 days into 7th month fetal blood changes so that it can carry it's own oxygen.	Redemption	**Blood** Hemoglobin A
Tabernacles End of Feasts Leviticus 23:27 15th day of 7th month Normal baby has 2 healthy lungs	**Kingdom** House of Spirit Spirit in the Air	**Lungs** Baby will live if born at Tabernacles

Hanukkah	**Eternity**	**Eternal Life**

Not given by God. A days' supply of oil lasted 8 nights. It's beyond Tabernacles and beyond the Kingdom. We have eternity with God. This is the fulfillment.

Job 23:12 ;

12 "I don't withdraw from his lips' command; I treasure his words more than my daily food."

Ecclesiastes 12:13;

13 Now all has been heard; here is the conclusion of the matter: Fear God and keep his commandments, for this is the duty of all mankind. (NIV®)

Made in the USA
Charleston, SC
01 June 2016